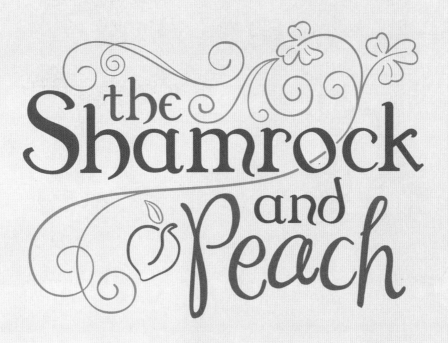

the Shamrock and Peach

by Judith McLoughlin

PHOTOGRAPHY
Gary McLoughlin

DESIGN BY
Gary McLoughlin
&
David Siglin

FOREWORDS BY
Chef Ford Fry
&
Chef Neven Maguire

Dunluce Castle, County Antrim

The Shamrock and Peach

A Culinary Journey from the North of Ireland to the American South

© 2011 by Judith McLoughlin
www.shamrockandpeach.com

Second Edition © 2016 by Judith McLoughlin
Printed in China

ISBN: 978-1-93550-780-2
eISBN: 978-1-62020-091-9

Cover Design by Gary McLoughlin
Page Layout by Gary McLoughlin & David Siglin
Photography by Gary McLoughlin

AMBASSADOR INTERNATIONAL
Emerald House
411 University Ridge, Suite B14
Greenville, SC 29601, USA
www.ambassador-international.com

AMBASSADOR BOOKS
The Mount
2 Woodstock Link
Belfast, BT6 8DD, Northern Ireland, UK
www.ambassador-international.com

The colophon is a trademark of Ambassador

American to metric Cooking Conversion Tables

The ingredients in this book are listed in American formats, such as 'cups' and 'ounces' (oz) but can be easily converted into the British equivalent using this chart. In my view the measurements for teaspoons and tablespoons are close enough not to worry about a conversion, but, it should be noted that an American pint measurement is *not* the same as a British pint, which is slightly larger. (1 US pint = .83 British pint/ 475 ml) I do hope this helps!

AMERICAN MEASUREMENT	METRIC EQUIVALENT
Fluid Measurements:	
1 tsp	5 ml
1 Tbsp	15ml
1 fl. oz.	28 ml
½ cup	120 ml
¾ cup	175 ml
1 cup	237 ml
1 pint	475 ml
Dry Measurements:	
1 oz	28 g
½ cup	115 g
¾ cup	175 g
1 cup	227 g
½ lb	227 g
1 lb	454 g

Oven Temperatures:

FAHRENHEIT	CELSIUS	GAS MARK
250 degrees F	120 degrees C	½
275 degrees F	130 degrees C	1
300 degrees F	150 degrees C	2
325 degrees F	165 degrees C	3
350 degrees F	180 degrees C	4
375 degrees F	190 degrees C	5
400 degrees F	200 degrees C	6
425 degrees F	220 degrees C	7
450 degrees F	230 degrees C	8
475 degrees F	245 degrees C	9

Scrabo Tower, County Down

Spanish moss, South Carolina

Introduction: Old and New Worlds Meet

There is just something about cooking and food, its smell and taste, its presentation and texture that brings families together around the table and sparks long evening conversations. A great meal cooked with loving care can make a house into a home and evoke memories of days long past as certain foods conjure up a place and a time. That first bite of a familiar food can no doubt put you thousands of miles away and bring a smile to your face.

This is especially true for those of us who, for many reasons, decided to pull up every root and replant ourselves in a different country across an ocean. For me, this uprooting meant leaving Northern Ireland while still in my twenties to embark on a journey of discovery with my new husband in America, the land of dreams and the resting place of many an uprooted Irish immigrant.

In the minds of most, the typical Irish immigrant seems rooted in the post–Civil War era of cities such as Boston or New York; and while these stereotypes are strong, they have served to obscure a much older tradition that preceded them by over a century, namely the Scots-Irish of the South. Otherwise known as the "Ulster-Scots," these people came predominantly from the northern province of Ulster in Ireland, the part of the island closest to Scotland. The Ulster-Scots folk who left the north of Ireland in the eighteenth century were mainly working-class Presbyterians who desired a land of freedom, wide-open spaces, and a place to call their own. At the time, persecution from the established church and strictly controlled land laws forced many of these resourceful people to sail the ocean and brave the frontier in the New World, which was no small task at the time. So, to the South they came by the thousands, bringing their unique food and culture with them. Bluegrass music, fiddle playing, square dancing, craft making, close-knit almost "clan-like" communities, and a deep sense of religiosity all came from the Scots-Irish traditions and are strongly apparent in the communities of the South today.

When my husband and I arrived in Georgia, we were at first bewildered by the culture. Very few people identified with the Irish, but we nonetheless found a strange familiarity with the place. I quickly identified with the deeply religious society and the warmth of Southern hospitality. After all, a church on every corner and a teacup in every hand was just like home! The Ulster culture was alive and well in the South, but few seemed to recognize the subtlety of it all. So, as we settled in Georgia, a blending of our cultures seemed natural and the pursuit of fusing Irish cooking with Southern hospitality inevitable.

I grew up in a family of wonderful cooks, continually surrounded by the inspiration of superb Irish food, so bringing a strong Irish culinary tradition with me to America to "comfort us" through the transition of immigration was completely natural. This was the inspiration behind the book you are now holding. The kitchen of my childhood was always filled with the scrumptious smells of farmhouse cooking. Whether it was fresh soda bread or roasting lamb, the memories are palatable, and my desire was always to continue these culinary traditions in my newly adopted land.

I hope in some way this introduction sets the scene for the novelty of the food and fun found within this book. An Irish kitchen in the Deep South, turning comfort food into an art form to be enjoyed at any time and used with great effect when entertaining, fusing Scots-Irish food with Southern culture, blending the old with the new.

So, please come with me on this journey of discovery from the winding roads and hedgerows of Northern Ireland to the antebellum finery of the South, and we'll discover a new twist on food that I know you will enjoy over and over again.

A View from the South

Foreword by Chef Ford Fry, Atlanta Georgia

Living and working with good food in the South has always felt very natural to me as a chef and restaurateur. That overarching sense of Southern hospitality invades everyday life, even in urban areas such as Atlanta, and makes what I do all the more fun. It seems as if people in the South are somehow engineered for sharing good times and food with those around them. We just love our family get-togethers and backyard barbeques that are overflowing with all kinds of interesting cooked creations, and perhaps that culture does indeed come from the Scots-Irish, as my friend Judith has suggested. Our Southern way of life is ingrained in us so deeply that many people don't stop and think about where all these roots spring from, or indeed where the origins of many of our Southern food traditions come from. So it is a pleasure for me to be involved with a timely cook book project such as Judith's *The Shamrock & Peach* that reaches back to those Southern and Irish commonalities and celebrates them in some way.

I have found it so interesting to consider our common heritage and see it come to life in this book in the language of really good food. As a chef, I'm passionate about creating culinary experiences in the Southern tradition using the choicest local ingredients yet with European techniques, and in so doing creating the best of both worlds at my restaurant in Atlanta. In many ways, Judith is reaching for a similar goal with her Irish cooking techniques applied to many Southern dishes using local produce readily available here in Georgia.

I wish Judith every success with this interesting book project as she brings a little bit of Ireland to us here in the South!

Chef Ford Fry
JCT Kitchen & Bar, Atlanta, Georgia

A View from the North

Foreword by Chef Neven Maguire, County Cavan

On a recent visit to the States, I met with Judith McLoughlin and was truly inspired by her passion, creativity, and love for Irish food! Judith grew up in an area not too far from where my restaurant is located, and it gives me great pleasure to feature one of my signature dishes in her cookbook, *The Shamrock & Peach*.

Cooking has always been a passion of mine. From a very young age, my favorite pastime was to shadow my mother in the kitchen, watching her cook; I soon began experimenting with ingredients in the home kitchen at the tender age of ten. My passion only intensified as I got older and, I have to say, I absolutely love what I do—to me, it's all about sharing my love for food with as many people as possible.

In Ireland, as in every country, we have our own unique recipes and cooking traditions, many of which are featured in Judith's cookbook; however, our cooking is also influenced by tastes and ingredients from across the globe. This fusion of Irish and continental/Asian cooking styles has produced a fantastic food culture in Ireland that is hard to beat!

We're also very fortunate to have great local resources and natural ingredients. In my restaurant, MacNean House, we source all our ingredients from local producers and insist on full traceability of all products used. This ensures only the highest quality dishes are served to our guests; we're delighted to have been honored with distinguished guests including Ireland's President Mary MacAlesse and Irish Actor Liam Neeson. The restaurant is also frequented regularly by journalists and food critics including Brendan O'Connor, Georgina Campbell, and John McKenna. This certainly keeps me on my toes!

On a final note, what I love about Judith's cookbook is that she successfully combines wonderful Irish and Southern American recipes and influences. The range and creativity of recipes in this cookbook will appeal to a broad range of cooks—at all levels. I wish Judith the very best of success with her latest venture, and I look forward to welcoming her to my own restaurant, MacNean House, if she is ever visiting Blacklion in County Cavan!

Chef Neven Maguire
MacNean House Restaurant, County Cavan

the Irish Heritage

The gatepost of the home I grew up in, in County Armagh, Northern Ireland. Surrounded by love & filled with the inspiration of my wonderful family.

Hillsborough, County Down

The road my grandparents walked

The Mourne Mountains

My father and mother

My Irish Heritage: Where It All Began

I believe that every person is living out the legacy left behind by another; the person you are today was shaped by the lives of another generation, and my story is not any different. As I look back over my life, I can see the clear hand of several generations of faithful family in play—my Irish heritage.

As someone who did not grow up in America but just landed as an adult in the country and culture, there are many things I have observed, many facets of culture that seem perfectly normal to everyone but stand out as a little unusual to my Irish eyes. One such observation is the almost universal interest in belonging and family roots: genealogy, if you will.

This great country is a vast melting pot of subcultures and peoples, a land of immigrants past, and it seems that almost everyone is from "somewhere else." Quite often when folks meet me for the first time, this interest is played out in the eagerness of people to explore and toast their Irish roots. It may be a grandmother who hailed from County Cork many moons ago or an explanation of an obscure surname and its Irish beginnings; and, you know, I actually love this American pursuit. To me it is a healthy thing. It's good to know where you came from and in so doing appreciate what you have and where you are going! A common heritage can bring a connection between utter strangers, and, if we add food into the equation, we have a winning combination. Food has a way of connecting people to their heritage, to a culture and to a time and place. Each culture has a range of foods that conjure up something unique about that culture and this is certainly true for Ireland. Beyond the cliché of boiled potatoes and corn beef the Scots-Irish heritage has a rich culinary story which is worth telling and I hope this book will go some way to advance that cause.

So it seems to me that food, culture, and heritage all complement and reinforce each other, and as such the recipes and hospitality ideas you will find in this chapter of *The Shamrock & Peach* are inspired by my past.

My romance with the art of hospitality and my deep love for cooking began its own journey many years ago in the life and experiences of my grandmother, who lived in a time when the dinner table was the benchmark of being together and was the centerpiece of the family. In the southeast corner of the province of Ulster lies the picturesque Kingdom of Mourne, an incredibly beautiful range of highlands that may have inspired C. S. Lewis as he dreamt of the geography of Narnia. Majestic and ancient mountains sweep right down into the Irish Sea, and it was here, in the small seaside resort of Newcastle, that my grandparents opened a bed and breakfast inn, naming it Tyrone House.

Situated in a long row of similarly Victorian terraced houses, it claimed a truly beautiful Irish setting with the flowing foam of the Irish Sea stretching out before it. With its beautiful setting on the promenade, it is no surprise that my grandparents were always busy and Tyrone House was always filled to capacity. Streams of visitors arrived by train from Belfast, coming in the summer months to stay in this much sought-after friendly guesthouse with its unique atmosphere, food, and location. This is where my love for food began, in the mind and heart of an Irish woman who dreamt of opening a guesthouse by the sea in County Down, a lady who longed to serve others and show her special brand of love through wonderful food brought to a table and enjoyed by stranger and friend alike. This love of hospitality was then in turn passed on to my mother and my aunt, and eventually to my sisters and me—three generations of Irish cooks.

So please enjoy these wonderfully Irish recipes that are drawn from the deep well of my heritage as I have looked back to the ideals taught and handed down to me by my family in Northern Ireland.

Scots-Irish Armagh oatmeal
served with Armagh apples, toasted walnuts and a creamed Irish whiskey sauce (serves 4)

The Story:

Eaten by Irish folks for many thousands of years, Ireland's most celebrated grain is also great for your health. Perhaps those ancient Celts were onto something? Turns out that oats contain a certain kind of fiber that lowers cholesterol in addition to providing us with vitamins, minerals and many antioxidants. Not so bad. Try adding toasted walnuts, a rich source of omega-3 fatty acids along with vitamin packed cranberries for that fusion powered punch to start your day with a bang!

So, now that we're feeling so good about the health benefits, let's add a wee drop of sweet whiskey sauce and some delicious red apple, famous in County Armagh, to take this Irish breakfast to a whole new level.

Enjoy!

Oatmeal ingredients

- 7 oz (1 cup) steel cut Irish oats
- 1 pint (2 cups) spring water
- 1 pint (2 cups) milk
- 1 tsp. salt
- 1 apple (chopped with skins on)
- 2 ½ oz toasted walnuts (chopped)

Whiskey Cream Sauce ingredients:

- 6 oz. (¾ cup) butter
- 5 oz. (3/4 cup) granulated sugar
- 2 tsp. water
- 1 egg yolk (beaten)
- 1 tsp. vanilla
- 3 Tbsp. Irish Whiskey
- 2 Tbsp. heavy whipping cream

How to make it:

1. Bring water, milk and salt to simmering point in a medium heavy based saucepan. Slowly stir in the steel cut oats, sprinkling lightly so the grains do not stick together in clumps.
2. Stir with a wooden spoon until the oatmeal begins to thicken. After about 5 minutes, reduce the heat to low. Simmer for 25 minutes or until oatmeal is cooked, remembering to stir several times. Add chopped apple and cook for 2-3 more minutes
3. To make the whiskey sauce combine the butter, water and sugar in a medium heavy based saucepan and stir on low heat until the sugar has dissolved. Remove from heat and slowly whisk in the beaten egg yolk, whiskey, vanilla and heavy whipping cream.
4. Strain sauce into a wee jug.
5. To enjoy the traditional way, serve the porridge steaming hot in small individual bowls with the whiskey sauce and toasted walnuts on top.

Classic Ulster Fry Stack

with portabella mushrooms and spring onion potato bites

The Story:

The famous Ulster Fry is one of the most celebrated dishes associated with Northern Ireland. Cooked Irish breakfasts are known throughout the world, but the Ulster Fry is a northern regional version that differs with the inclusion of soda bread and potato bread and may include white and black pudding. The fry is typically served for breakfast but is also enjoyed at any time of the day throughout Northern Ireland. Go to any pub or tearoom in Belfast and beyond, and the Ulster Fry will be an essential menu item. In fact, if you spend any amount of time in Ulster, you will quickly discern that this dish is part of the fabric of our culture!

For this recipe, though, I have taken the dish up a notch or two by adding portabella mushrooms for the base of the stack, as well as substituting spring onion potato bites for the more traditional potato farls. I hope you'll enjoy it!

Ingredients (serves 4):

- 1 Tbsp. vegetable oil
- 4 slices of bacon
- 3 Tbsp. brown sugar
- 4 large Irish breakfast sausages or 8 small links
- 4 portabella mushrooms
- 4 free range eggs
- 1 large beef tomato (cut into 4 thick slices)
- Sea salt and pepper
- 12 spring onion potato bread bites (*see "Bakery" chapter*)
- 2 Tbsp. parsley (finely chopped)

How to make it:

1. To make the spring onion potato bread, follow the recipe from the "Bakery" chapter, folding in chopped spring onions. Roll out to ¼" depth with a floured rolling pin and cut with a 1" biscuit cutter.
2. To make the *brown sugar bacon*, preheat the oven to 425° F and place the slices on a foil-lined baking sheet, on one layer.
3. Bake in oven for 12 minutes until *slightly* crispy.
4. Turn over each slice of bacon and sprinkle with brown sugar.
5. Bake for 5 more minutes until crispy with the fat turning golden brown.
6. Transfer to a warm plate.
7. Add a little vegetable oil to the pan and fry the sausages on medium-high heat turning to brown and cook on all sides.
8. Add the portabella mushrooms to the skillet and cook for 5–6 minutes, turning once.
9. In a clean skillet, add a little vegetable oil and place on medium heat. Crack the eggs carefully into the pan and add a little water to *steam* them a little.
10. Continue to cook for about 2 minutes for *sunny side up*, or turn if you like them *over easy*.
11. Transfer to a warm plate.
12. Add a small amount of oil and sauté tomatoes for 30 seconds on each side. Season with salt and freshly ground pepper.
13. To assemble stack, place the sautéed portabella mushroom in the center of plate then stack the beef, tomato, fried egg, sausage, and brown sugar bacon on top. Garnish with a little parsley.
14. Place three pieces of spring onion potato bread in a triangle outside the stack circle.

Traditional Scots Cock-a-Leekie Soup

The story:

Few Scottish recipes date back as far as this traditional soup, which can be traced all the way to the sixteenth century, a time of kilts, castles, and roaring fires, a period when the Scots were frequently going back and forth to Ulster. This is an ancient recipe, but I have given this old bird a new twist with some modern flavors to enliven the experience! A version of this soup was always cooking on the Aga cooking stove when I was growing up and must be one of the most popular farmhouse favorites throughout Northern Ireland. Sometimes my mother would replace the rice with barley, and the family recipe did not include prunes, but most other ingredients are true to tradition.

Soup ingredients:

- 10 dried plumbs or prunes (6 oz.)
- 1 small chicken (3 lbs. washed with giblets removed)
- 6 medium-sized leeks (2 lbs. washed and chopped)
- 2 oz. long grain rice (washed)
- 3 medium carrots (grated)
- water to cover chicken (6 pints)
- bouquet garni (thyme sprigs, sage, bay leaves)
- 2 tsp. salt
- ½ tsp. freshly milled black pepper
- 4 slices smoked bacon

Parsley Purée ingredients:

- 1 bunch flat leaf parsley (1 cup with stems removed)
- 2 medium garlic cloves
- 1 oz. "Ivernia" Irish cheese or parmesan (grated)
- 4 fl. oz. (½ cup) olive oil
- zest of one lemon
- 1 tsp. kosher salt

How to make it:

1. Soak dried plumbs or prunes overnight in cold water.
2. In a medium-sized saucepan, add the chicken, half of the leeks, 1 slice of the smoky bacon, the bouquet garni, and enough water to cover the bird. Bring to a boil and simmer for 2½ hours until the meat is falling off the bone.
3. Strain the stock into a clean pot. Remove the chicken meat from the bones and discard everything else. Add the remaining leeks, grated carrots, and dried plumbs or prunes. Cook for 20 more minutes. Remove from heat and add a portion of the cooked chicken, very finely chopped. Taste to adjust seasoning, adding salt and pepper as necessary.
4. Prepare purée by placing parsley, garlic, and cheese with lemon zest in the food processor, slowly drizzling olive oil in to make a paste. Sauté remaining slices of bacon until crispy and chop finely.
5. Serve in warmed bowls, using a fork to swirl a little parsley purée on top with sprinkles of the bacon.

Griddle Boxty BLT Bites
with smoked bacon, lettuce, and roasted tomato

The Story:

Boxty is said to have originated in County Fermanagh in Northern Ireland, and I have some old recipes from my grandmother where the dumplings were made by boiling raw *and* mashed potatoes, *then* frying them in the pan. The old-fashioned griddle was placed over the fire in Ulster homes, and "Boxty" bread would slowly bake on the flame-heated iron surface. As the old Irish saying goes, "Boxty on the griddle, Boxty in the pan, if you cannot make Boxty, you'll never get a man."

Boxty BLT bites ingredients (allow 3–4 per guest):
- 24 potato bread rounds (*see "Bakery" chapter*)
- 12 roasted red tomato halves (cut in half)
- 1 bunch Arugula leaves (stems removed)
- 1 tsp. olive oil
- kosher salt and ground black pepper (to season)
- 8 slices thick cut smoked bacon (cooked and cut into 3 pieces)
- 2 fl. oz. (¼ cup) mayonnaise

Roasted red tomatoes ingredients:
- 6 Roma tomatoes (cut lengthwise)
- ½ tsp. sea salt
- ¼ tsp. pepper
- chopped fresh herbs (parsley, thyme)
- 1 Tbsp. good quality olive oil
- ½ tsp. sugar (to sprinkle)

How to make them:
1. Preheat oven to 250° F.
2. Toss tomatoes in olive oil and season well with sea salt, pepper, sugar, and herbs. Place tomatoes face-side up on a baking pan and slowly roast for 1½–2 hours. Remove from the oven and allow to cool.
3. Follow the instructions for *classic potato cheese bread*.
4. Roll out to ¼" depth with a floured rolling pin and cut with a 1" biscuit cutter.
5. Fry bacon in a large heavy-based skillet until crispy and set aside on a warmed plate.
6. Sprinkle a little flour on griddle and cook Boxty bread bites in small batches on medium heat for 3–4 minutes on each side until the crust is golden brown.
7. To assemble bites, begin by slicing bacon into thirds and dressing Arugula with a little olive oil, salt, and pepper. Place a small dollop of mayonnaise on top of the Boxty bread, followed by the Arugula leaves, smoked bacon, and the sliced roasted tomatoes.

Irish Spring Lamb Stew

with fresh parsley and rosemary sea salt

The Story:

There is nothing as quintessentially Irish as a lamb stew, essential to the menus of a thousand Irish pubs and a part of our weekly diet growing up on the farm in Northern Ireland. I also *love* "one pot meals" such as these, as they can be prepared the day before, helping moms with busy schedules. It's also a superb family meal as the "shoulder chop," used for the lamb ingredient, is generally an economical cut of meat. Adding the potatoes in two batches allows first for the stew to thicken and second to stay in chunks.

I serve my version of this classic Irish stew with my own rosemary sea salt, which adds just the right amount of flavoring and seasoning to take this dish from great to perfect!

Ingredients (serves 4):

- 2 lbs. of gigot or shoulder lamb chops (bone-in)
- kosher salt and freshly ground black pepper
- 2 Tbsp. flour
- 2 Tbsp. olive oil
- 2 lbs. (about 6 medium potatoes peeled and diced into 1" chunks)
- 2 medium onions (finely chopped)
- 4 medium carrots (peeled and cut into 1½" chunks)
- 16 fl. oz. (2 cups) water

Condiments:

- rosemary salt (1 Tbsp. sea salt to 1 tsp. finely chopped rosemary)
- parsley (finely chopped)
- olive oil (to drizzle)

How to make it:

1. Peel and dice the potatoes and carrots. Place in a bowl of cold, salted water.
2. Preheat the oven to 350° F.
3. Trim off any visible fat from the lamb chops.
4. Combine the flour, salt, and pepper in a bowl and coat the chops in flour mixture.
5. Heat the oil in a large, ovenproof skillet and braise the chops in small batches. When done, transfer the meat to the base of an ovenproof dish.
6. Sauté the onions in the same skillet as used to braise the lamb for 3–4 minutes to soften and lightly caramelize.
7. Transfer the onion and half of the potatoes on top of the meat.
8. Cover with water and bake for 1½ hours.
9. Add the carrots and the rest of the potatoes. Simmer with the dish covered for an additional 30 minutes until the vegetables are tender.
10. To serve, remove the bones from the chops and stir the meat and vegetables together. Place in individual bowls and garnish with rosemary sea salt, chopped parsley, and a drizzle of olive oil.

Beef with Irish Stout and Parsley Dumplings

The Story:

This wonderful recipe has proved to be my signature dish for the Ulster Kitchen, and I have made this Irish delight for numerous parties, formal cooking classes, and even on various TV cooking shows. Everyone just seems to love it, as the beef goes incredibly well with Irish stout. The flavors are almost made for each other. Oh, and I should also mention that stout is good for you, so you can actually feel *good* about this hearty dish as you take in the warm aroma of it cooking slowly with the flavorful beef. Serve over a helping of "Champ" potatoes and you have a winner!

The idea for this dish came to me from my aunt in Northern Ireland, Anne Ringland, who spent a lifetime as a culinary teacher and kindly imparted this recipe idea to me. She is a superb cook herself, as this page will testify to!

Beef and stout ingredients (serves 4–6):

- 2 lbs. beef chuck mock tender cut
- (cut into 1½" cubes)
- 1½ tsp. sea salt
- ½ tsp. ground black pepper
- 2 fl. oz. (¼ cup) olive oil
- 2 medium onions (peeled and chopped)
- 3 Tbsp. flour (blended in a little water)
- 16 fl. oz. (2 cups) Irish stout
- 4 fl. oz. (½ cup) beef stock
- bouquet garni (tied sprig of thyme, rosemary, bay leaves, and sage)
- 2 cloves garlic (crushed)
- 2 tsp. sugar
- 1 medium leek (cut in thin strips)
- 2 carrots (cut in thin strips)

Parsley dumplings ingredients:

- 5½ oz. (1¼ cups) self-rising flour
- 2 oz (¼ cup) butter (cold)
- 3 Tbsp. parsley (chopped)
- 2 fl. oz. (¼ cup) iced water
- salt and pepper (to taste)

How to make it:

1. Preheat oven to 350° F, cube the meat and sprinkle with plenty of salt and pepper. Begin to brown the meat in hot oil in small batches, transferring each batch to a Dutch oven when done.
2. Sauté the onions in a skillet until they are lightly colored. Transfer to the Dutch oven with the meat.
3. Deglaze the sauté pan with a little Irish stout and pour over the meat and onions, adding the rest of the stout, blended flour mixture, beef stock, garlic, sugar, and bouquet garni.
4. Cover the casserole and place in the oven for 2 hours or until the meat is very tender.
5. While casserole is baking, prepare the dumplings by measuring the flour and salt, mixing them with the butter until it resembles breadcrumbs. Stir in the parsley and season. Add water to form the dough and shape into 12 small balls in the palm of your hand.
6. Remove the casserole from the oven, discard the bouquet garni, and quickly drop the dumplings on top of the casserole while it is still bubbling. Return it to the oven uncovered and bake for a further 20–25 minutes.
7. Blanch the leeks and carrots in boiling water for 1 minute then transfer to a bowl of iced water. Gently sauté for a garnish.
8. Serve on top of Irish "Champ" potatoes, garnishing with the leek and carrot julienne.

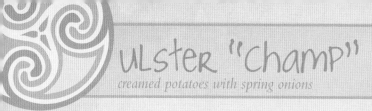

ulster "champ"
creamed potatoes with spring onions

The story:

"Champ" is an old Northern Irish tradition, fondly eaten and cherished by generations of Ulster folk, and, as with many traditional regional dishes, great variations exist from family to family. Some add eggs, some don't. Some add cream, some don't, and so on.

For this particular recipe, I have also created yet another variation on this beloved dish, calling it "Green Champ," which seems entirely fitting for this Irish cookbook. Enjoy!

Ingredients:

- 2½ lbs. potatoes (floury variety)
- 1 bunch (1 cup) green onions (chopped)
- 4 fl. oz. (½ cup) heavy whipping cream
- 4 fl. oz. (½ cup) milk
- 4 oz. (½ cup) unsalted butter
- 1 tsp. sea salt
- ½ tsp. ground black pepper

How to make it:

1. Peel and quarter potatoes. Place them in a large pan and cook in enough cold water to cover the potatoes for 30 minutes or until tender.
2. Drain the potatoes, cover the pan, and allow them to dry for a few minutes.
3. While the potatoes are still cooking, combine 2 oz of butter, the heavy whipping cream, and milk, bringing them to a boil.
4. Remove from heat and stir in the spring onions, giving them a few minutes to infuse.
5. Mash the potatoes and gently stir in the cream mixture with the salt and pepper to make a smooth consistency.
6. Serve in a warm serving bowl, making a shallow hole in the center of the potatoes with the back of a spoon.
7. Fill with the remaining 2 oz. of melted butter and serve immediately.

How to make the Green Champ variation (add these steps to above instructions):

1. Blanch one bunch (1 cup) of green onions in a pan of boiling water and quickly transfer to a bowl of ice water to keep the vibrant green color.
2. Chop the green onions and then purée them in a food processor.
3. Slowly combine heavy cream, milk, and melted butter to the green onion purée.
4. Run the cooked potatoes through a ricer or food mill and then fold in the green onion purée mixture to make a smooth consistency. with fresh parsley and rosemary sea salt

white Chocolate Bread and Butter Pudding
with a warm Irish cream custard

The Story:

Always an old Irish favorite, the Bread and Butter Pudding goes back many generations and was for many farmhouse cooks an ingenious way of using up the leftovers from the week's baking. These days, however, we make the dessert not out of necessity but out of pure indulgence, as this recipe will prove to you. Here I have taken the traditional recipe and enriched it with white chocolate. Serve with the custard sauce and you will have a winner, believe me. The aroma in your kitchen will be a delight to the family, and the dessert goes particularly well with an Irish coffee. You could also try this sauce over apple pie for an alternative treat.

Pudding ingredients:

- 1 loaf of Irish tea bread (*see "Bakery" chapter*)
- 2 oz. (¼ cup) butter
- 4 eggs (beaten)
- 8 fl. oz. (1 cup) whole milk
- 8 fl. oz. (1 cup) heavy whipping cream
- 8 oz. (1 1/3 cups) white chocolate
- 2 oz. (¼ cup) sugar
- freshly grated nutmeg

Irish cream custard sauce ingredients (makes 2 cups):

- 16 fl. oz. (2 cups) heavy whipping cream
- 4 egg yolks (beaten)
- 4 oz. (½ cup) sugar
- 2 fl. oz. (¼ cup) Irish cream

How to make it:

1. Butter a medium 9" baking dish.
2. Slice and butter the tea bread, then cut into triangles. Layer the bread in a pan and set aside.
3. Break up the white chocolate into a double boiler, combining the cream, milk, sugar, and chocolate, then stir until chocolate has melted. Set aside to cool slightly.
4. Beat eggs and briskly incorporate them into the Irish cream chocolate mixture. Pour evenly over buttered tea bread and grate fresh nutmeg on top of the pudding. Cover and soak overnight in the refrigerator.
5. Preheat the oven to 325° and then bake for 35–40 minutes or until the center is set and is firm to the touch.

How to make the custard sauce:

1. Pour cream into a saucepan and heat on medium low until simmering. Remove from heat.
2. In a separate bowl, beat egg yolks and sugar for 1–2 minutes or until pale yellow in color. Gradually whisk the warm cream into the egg yolk mixture until fully incorporated. Place saucepan back on medium low heat and stir with a wooden spoon for a few minutes until the custard is thick enough to coat the back of the spoon. Be careful not to allow the sauce to boil or it will curdle.
3. Remove from heat and strain into a clean bowl. Stir in Irish cream.
4. Serve right away by pooling the custard on the plate, add the pudding bread, and drizzle with custard. If making ahead of time, cover surface of custard with plastic wrap to prevent a skin forming. Remember: heat *slowly* if you need to reheat the custard.

Scots-Irish Oaten Raspberry Cranachan

The Story:

This dessert is a traditional Highland delight typically served in Scotland at the New Year and at "Burns Night" suppers. Scottish Cranachan may also be known as "Cream Crowdie" and is traditionally made with wild heather honey and whiskey folded into the fresh cream and oats. To liven it up here, though, I decided to add whiskey to the raspberries, and white chocolate to the cream for that Scots-Irish taste of indulgence. Serve in tall glasses with long silver spoons and try dipping some shortbread or flake-meal cookies into the creamy dessert to finish it off.

Ingredients:

- 3 oz. (1/3 cup) Scots or Irish steel cut oats
- 2 Tbsp. light brown sugar
- 1 Tbsp. butter
- 12 fl. oz. (1½ cup) heavy whipped cream
- 6 large squares (5 oz.) quality white chocolate
- 3 Tbsp. Scotch or Irish whiskey
- 10 oz. (just under 2 cups) raspberries
- 2 Tbsp. local honey

How to make it:

1. In large skillet toast the oats with the brown sugar and butter, stirring constantly to avoid burning. Set aside to cool.
2. In a blender, purée half of the raspberries and strain to remove seeds.
3. Fold the remaining raspberries into the purée (reserving a few to garnish) and stir in the whiskey and honey.
4. In a small saucepan over a low heat, bring ½ cup of heavy whipping cream to simmering point (do not boil) and slowly incorporate the white chocolate into the cream, stopping to beat with each addition until smooth. Cool to room temperature.
5. Beat the remaining 1 cup of cream until *soft peaks* appear, then fold in the white chocolate cream and toasted oats.
6. In a tall glass, layer the raspberry purée with white chocolate cream mixture. Top with the raspberry purée and end with cream.
7. Garnish with a single raspberry, shavings of white chocolate, toasted oats, and a sprig of mint.
8. Serve immediately, as the oats can become soft and lose their crunch.

Contented sheep, Stramore Farm

My boys, Peter & Jack, Stramore Farm

the Irish farm

Stramore Farm, Northern Ireland. A place of fond memories, wholesome ingredients and some of the best farmhouse cooking in Ulster!

Cattle grazing, County Down

Our Ulster farmhouse in Northern Ireland

Ancient ivy lined walls lead to the farm

Old stone fort in the walls of our farm

I grew up and spent my formative years surrounded by the rolling green fields of an Irish farm set deep in the Ulster countryside in County Armagh. Our neighbors grew vegetables and potatoes in the rich, dark soil while my father raised plump, white sheep and sturdy, young cattle for market. The stone walls that enclosed the acreage of our farm were built in the seventeenth century. They were thick with waxy ivy and rough with age. The centuries of wind and rain had formed a beauty all their own on the old enclosures, a character that is found and formed only in old places. The farm buildings were built of stacked stone with red metal roofs and echoed of times long past. It's the kind of environment that stirs a deep love of the land in your heart and never lets you go.

As a cook obsessed with all the varieties of ingredients found on the farm, I realized from an early age just how good farm-fresh food really is. Our fast-paced society has tried to rob us of the wholesomeness of good food, but once tasted, the experience is never forgotten. The old is becoming new again as we strive for organic and healthy farm-fresh food in the midst of the mediocre.

Each year thousands of tourists flock to Ireland, not for the bright lights or the glitz of urban pleasures but mostly for the almost lost euphoria of being close to the land—to be in a sparsely populated, green country where rural folks value the land lovingly and ensure that their rivers, lakes, fields, and hedgerows are clean and unpolluted. They come to fish and to walk, to cycle in the little lanes that snake throughout the countryside, and to breathe in the air free from the city grime so many in our world never question.

In this chapter I want to bring you back to the green fields of Northern Ireland and to introduce you to some of my favorite farm recipes that I cherished and enjoyed growing up. All of the recipes in this chapter use ingredients that are common to Irish farms, such as hormone-free beef from grass fed cattle, or free-range duck, or delicious root vegetables, or blackberries picked from the hedgerows. The recipes are traditional yet fresh with great ingredients that make all the difference. In fact, my best meal experiences always take me back to the simple pleasures I enjoyed in my mother's farmhouse kitchen: the smell of roast beef crackling and hissing in the Aga stove or a hearty soup stirring in the pot, ready for the farm workers coming up to the kitchen, fresh from cutting silage that kept our cattle fed over the winter. The farm laborers always loved our farm kitchen and no one ever left the table hungry, believe me.

Today in Atlanta and indeed across America, the "farm to table" movement has really gained momentum, and as I alluded to earlier, it's easy to see why. In urban America many people are finding themselves a world away from the land, locked into gray city settings or sprawling suburban landscapes void of farming. We browse the aisles of our supermarkets almost overwhelmed by the amount of food available in bright and colorful packaging, entirely unaware of how this food got here. To most urban dwellers in the 21st century farms seem nostalgic and somehow unreal, but with a larger emphasis on health and well-being people are at last beginning to take an interest in where their food originates and from a cook's perspective, this is a very good thing. After all, if people demand fresh ingredients, an interest in how to cook them will rise right alongside that demand.

Sometimes the best food may not be fancy but earthy and simple. This sums up where we are going with this chapter: simple recipes that are defined by their flavor and wholesome ingredients rather than by chic presentation. So please take a journey with me to the farm in Northern Ireland and the great food prepared with loving care by wonderful farmhouse cooks such as my mother. This is farm-fresh food with a story to tell!

Ulster Cream of Vegetable Soup

The story:

This wholesome root vegetable soup uses all the key ingredients that grow locally in rural Ireland but are also found everywhere in the United States. A true Ulster farmhouse recipe, this soup will warm you and revive you with its wholesome ingredients, many of which people are now growing organically in their own kitchen gardens.

One of the greatest compliments I have ever received as a professional cook was when I served this soup at a luncheon in Atlanta. A guest at the luncheon, who was originally from Belfast, suddenly burst into tears following the first course and announced to me that "this tastes like home." Truly, this soup is the taste of rural Northern Ireland.

Ingredients (serves 4):

- 3 Tbsp. butter
- 1 medium onion (1 cup) finely chopped
- 1 large leek (1 cup) washed and chopped
- 1 potato (1 cup) cubed
- 2 medium carrots (1½ cups) peeled and chopped
- 2 pints (4 cups) chicken or vegetable stock
- 2 fl. oz. (¼ cup) whipping cream
- 1 Tbsp. parsley (chopped)
- ½ tsp. kosher salt
- ¼ tsp. ground black pepper

How to make it:

1. In a large soup pot, melt the butter and sauté the onions and leeks for about 5 minutes until the onions are translucent.
2. Add the carrots and potato. Continue to *sweat* the vegetables for about 8 minutes until they are fragrant and soft.
3. Add the stock and salt and pepper. Bring the soup to a boil and then cover with a lid, reducing temperature to medium.
4. Cook for about 10 minutes until all the vegetables are tender.
5. Remove the soup from the heat and cool slightly in saucepan.
6. Purée the soup with hand blender or in batches using a food processor.
7. Bring the soup back to a slow boil and then switch to low heat before adding the whipping cream. Adjust the seasoning to taste.
8. Garnish each serving with some fresh chopped parsley.

farmhouse ulster Broth

with braised beef & winter vegetables

The story:

My mother used to make this hearty dish at least once a week for us as I was growing up on the farm. It was a staple for feeding hungry agricultural workers who used to arrive at the farmhouse hungry and ready for lunch. A few times a year my father would contract men to help us make the silage we needed to keep our cattle fed over the winter months, and these hardy Irish men just loved bowl after bowl. The mighty combine harvester would cut the summer growth grass at record speed and the men would say that they *always* looked forward to working on our farm simply because of my mother's amazing Ulster broth. Sometimes also known as *Scotch broth*, this dish is the taste of rural Ulster!

Ulster broth ingredients:

- 1½ lbs. beef chuck mock tenderloin (cut in ¾" cubes)
- 2 Tbsp. olive oil
- 1 Tbsp. butter
- 1 large onion (chopped)
- 1 large leek (cleaned and chopped)
- 3 pints (6 cups) vegetable stock
- ½ small yellow turnip or rutabaga (2 cups peeled and cubed)
- 4 medium potatoes (2 cups peeled and diced)
- 5 medium-sized carrots (1½ cups peeled and diced)
- 6 Tbsp. pearl barley
- 3 Tbsp. parsley (chopped)
- salt and pepper to season

How to make it:

1. Presoak the barley in plenty of cold water for at least 1 hour, or overnight.
2. Season the beef with salt and pepper to prepare.
3. Heat the olive oil in large sauté pan and sear the meat in small batches for just a few minutes. Then transfer the meat to an ovenproof dish or a large saucepan.
4. Add the butter to the sauté pan and cook the onions and leeks for 3–4 minutes. Remove from the pan and add to meat in the ovenproof dish.
5. Pour the vegetable stock over the meat, onions, and leeks. Bring to a boil, then turn the temperature down to low and cook for 1½ hours.
6. While the beef is cooking, prepare the carrots and yellow turnip.
7. Add the pearl barley and cook for 15 minutes, then add the remaining vegetables. Cover and simmer for a further 25 minutes until all the vegetables are tender when pieced with a fork.
8. Skim off any fat from surface of broth. Season to taste.
9. Serve in a warmed soup bowl and garnish with chopped parsley.

Classic Ulster Shepherd's Pie

The Story:

This is another great Irish country dish that is economical and can feed a large crowd or family. When I was a child, it was a personal favorite of mine, and now that I have children of my own it has in turn become their firm favorite also. The simplicity of the potato topping combined with the tasty beef center is always a winning combination. No need to overcomplicate it; just enjoy this Old World classic as generations of British and Irish have and still do in pubs and clubs the length and breadth of the land. Serve with a mixed green salad or petite garden peas.

Meat layer ingredients:

- 2 lbs. quality hormone-free lean ground beef
- 2 Tbsp. olive oil
- 1 small onion (peeled and finely chopped)
- 1½ Tbsp. flour
- 12 fl. oz. (1½ cups) beef stock
- 2 small carrots (scraped and diced)
- 1 clove garlic (crushed)
- 1 Tbsp. tomato paste
- 2 Tbsp. Worcestershire sauce
- 1 tsp. salt and ¼ tsp. pepper
- 1 Tbsp. fresh thyme (chopped)
- 2 Tbsp. parsley (chopped for garnish)

Potato layer ingredients:

- 3 lbs. potatoes (floury variety peeled and cut into small pieces)
- 6 fl. oz. (¾ cup) half and half cream and milk
- 3 Tbsp. butter
- kosher salt and white pepper

How to make it:

1. In a large skillet heat the oil and sauté the onions for 5 minutes to soften but not to brown. Add in the meat in small batches, *then* braise until brown.
2. Stir in the flour and coat the meat mixture completely.
3. Add the beef stock, carrots, garlic, thyme, tomato paste, salt, pepper, and Worcestershire sauce. Cover and cook on low for about 45 minutes.
4. While the beef is cooking, prepare the topping by cooking the peeled potatoes in lightly salted water for about 20 minutes until soft when pierced with a fork.
5. Drain and mash the potatoes, mixing in the milk, butter, a pinch of salt, and a touch of white pepper.
6. To assemble the pie, spoon the meat into 6 individual dishes or a 9x13" casserole dish and top with the potato mixture. (For great presentation, swirl fork over potato in a zigzag fashion.)
7. Preheat the oven to 350°F and bake for 25 minutes.
8. Broil the potato for the last 2 minutes for a golden crust and garnish with some chopped parsley before serving with vegetables of your choice.

Neeps'n Tatties
mashed rutabaga (Irish turnip) and carrots with creamed potato

The story:

Scots-Irish folks love to mash their root vegetables, and when freshly dug from the earth, boiled, seasoned, and mashed, there are few more simple pleasures than these. A true comfort food that suits the colder climates in Scotland and Northern Ireland, this simple pairing will nevertheless work as a cold comfort in Appalachia also. Serve the Neeps'n Tatties mashed side by side either on their own or as a side dish.

Ingredients for the Neeps:
- 1 lb. turnip/rutabagas (peeled & cut into chunks)
- 1 lb. carrots (peeled and quartered)
- 2 Tbsp. unsalted butter
- 3 Tbsp. light cream
- ¼ tsp. nutmeg (good pinch)
- 1 Tbsp. parsley (chopped)
- ½ tsp. sea salt
- ¼ tsp. white pepper

Ingredients for the Tatties:
- 2 lbs. potatoes (floury variety peeled & quartered)
- 2 oz. unsalted butter
- 2 fl. oz (1/4 cup) light cream
- 1 Tbsp. chives (chopped)
- ½ tsp. sea salt
- ¼ tsp. ground black pepper

How to make the Neeps:
1. Prepare the turnip and carrots then cut into small even pieces.
2. Place the turnips in a pot of cold water and bring to a boil.
3. Cook for 10 minutes before adding the carrots.
4. Cook the vegetables together for a further 20–25 minutes until tender when pierced with a fork.
5. Drain the vegetables and mash them together.
6. Gently heat the milk and butter together, incorporate liquid with the vegetables, and stir in the parsley, nutmeg, salt, and pepper.

How to make the Tatties:
1. Prepare the potatoes and place in pot of cold water.
2. Bring to a boil and cook for 15–20 minutes until tender when pierced with a fork.
3. Drain and dry out by placing the potatoes in metal colander over a saucepan, allowing the heat to gently dry and steam them.
4. Warm the milk and add the butter.
5. Mash potatoes and add wet ingredients.
6. Stir in the chives, salt, and pepper.

Duck in a Honey & Wheat Beer Sauce
with sautéed spinach and ginger

The Story:

Duck, geese, and other game poultry were always on the menu at our farm, as our neighbors raised birds for market and for sport shooting, which is common in rural Ireland. We always loved the occasion of eating game birds, especially when enhanced with other flavors, and this recipe is a special treat to serve guests in your home. It always seems to impress. The honey and wheat beer together are a superb combination, as the sweetness of the honey complements the light, tart flavors of the wheat beer, and both blend together incredibly well with a gamy poultry such as duck. Try this one with some sautéed spinach, ginger, and pearl onions for an incredibly tasty dish.

Duck and Spinach ingredients:
- 4 duck breasts (boneless)
- 1 tsp. kosher salt
- ½ tsp. black pepper
- 2 Tbsp. vegetable oil
- 20 pearl onions
- 6–8 oz. fresh spinach (2 ½ cups)
- 1 tsp. fresh root ginger (grated)
- 2 Tbsp. butter

Honey and Beer Sauce ingredients:
- 1½ pints (3 cups) Irish Wheat Beer
- 2½ fl. oz. (1/3 cup) chicken stock
- 1 Tbsp. thyme (chopped)
- 6 Tbsp. honey (plus a little extra to glaze)
- 2 Tbsp. soy sauce
- salt and pepper (to taste)

How to make it:

1. Score the skin of the duck breasts with a sharp knife and season with sea salt and black pepper. Preheat oven to 425° F.
2. Quickly prepare the pearl onions by placing them in boiling water for 3 minutes, then rinse in cold water. Cut the ends off each pearl onion and remove the skin.
3. Heat the oil in a heavy, large skillet over high heat and add the pearl onions and prepared duck breasts, skin side down.
4. Sauté for 5 minutes until the skin is golden brown. Turn the duck breasts over and sear on the other side for a further 2 minutes.
5. Remove the onions from the skillet and set aside.
6. Place the skillet in a preheated oven and cook the duck for a further 5 minutes for *medium rare*, 10 minutes for *well done*.
7. Meanwhile, reduce the beer by two thirds (just less than 1 cup) by gently boiling.
8. Remove the duck from the oven and transfer to a cutting board to rest.
9. Drain off excess fat from the pan and deglaze with chicken stock. Combine the chicken stock, reduced beer, honey, soy sauce, and pearl onions, then bring to a boil, cooking for a further 2 minutes.
10. In another clean large skillet, melt the butter over medium heat, then add ginger and sauté for 1 minute. Add the spinach to the same skillet and sauté for 1 more minute.
11. Brush the duck breasts with a little extra honey and slice thinly.
12. To serve, place a small amount of spinach and ginger in the center of each plate. Place the sliced duck breasts and onions on top and drizzle with the sauce.

Ballybay fillet Mignon Steak
with creamed Irish whiskey mushrooms

The Story:

All good memories for me start with "Bally"! My grandparent's family home is called *Ballyworkan*, while another was *Ballywillwill*, and the *Ballybay* River ran through our hometown where the naturally grass-fed cattle were seen grazing and chewing their cud on warm summer days. In fact, it seems that most places in Northern Ireland start with a "Bally" of some sort, and the word graces the names of many a farm or townland across the province. So, this dish is a shout out to the farmers of Ulster in celebration of the goodness that is the stock of our high quality countryside.

Ingredients (serves 4):

- four 6 oz. fillet mignon steaks
- freshly ground black pepper and kosher salt
- 1 Tbsp. olive oil
- ½ small onion (finely chopped)
- 1½ Tbsp. flour
- 2 fl. oz. (¼ cup) cabernet sauvignon
- 6 fl. oz. (¾ cup) beef stock
- 6 turns of freshly ground black pepper
- 14 oz. mushrooms (wiped and chopped)
- 2 oz. (¼ cup) butter
- 3 Tbsp. whiskey
- 2 fl. oz. (¼ cup) heavy whipping cream
- kosher salt and freshly ground black pepper
- 1 tsp. freshly chopped thyme

How to make it:

1. Begin by seasoning the steaks with plenty of salt and freshly ground pepper.
2. Wipe and chop the mushrooms.
3. Melt the butter in a large medium-hot skillet and add the mushrooms. Sauté for 5–6 minutes until seared and golden brown.
4. Stir in the whiskey, standing back in case it flames. Allow alcohol to burn off a little before adding the cream, then season and stir in the thyme.
5. Preheat your oven to 400° F.
6. Sear the fillets in a little olive oil in a medium-high pan for 1 minute on each side, then transfer to the hot oven and cook for 5–6 minutes for *medium rare* and 8–9 minutes for *well done*. Remove from oven and transfer the steaks to a warm plate to rest.
7. To make the red wine reduction, sauté the onions in the same pan used to cook the steaks, then add the flour and cook for about 1 minute. Stir in the red wine and beef stock. Bring the sauce to a boil and simmer for 4–5 minutes. Season with plenty of black pepper and salt.
8. Pour any juices from the steaks into the red wine sauce so as not to waste a single drop of flavor, then reduce sauce again slightly before straining with a small sieve.
9. To serve, spoon a little of the red wine reduction on each plate. Place a fillet on the sauce and top with the whiskey mushrooms.

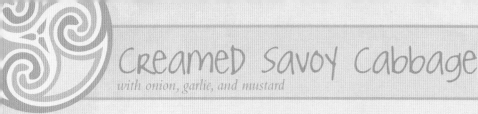

Creamed Savoy Cabbage
with onion, garlic, and mustard

The Story:

Savoy cabbage is a firm favorite throughout Ireland, nurtured in fields and gardens at every farmhouse the length and breadth of the country. It's easily grown in the Irish climate, and cabbage, as well as tasting great, is packed with nutrients, so it's no wonder it's an Irish favorite. My mother would often intensify the flavor by frying the cooked cabbage in some reserved bacon fat to create a simple dish bursting with flavor.

These days we may be a little more health-conscious and may not use so much bacon grease, so why not try this more sophisticated version of an Irish farmhouse classic, and you'll be hooked!

Ingredients:

- 1 Tbsp. olive oil
- 1 Tbsp. butter
- 1 medium onion (thinly sliced)
- 4 cloves garlic (finely sliced)
- 1 savoy cabbage (about 2 lbs. shredded)
- kosher salt and white pepper
- 2 fl. oz. (¼ cup) heavy cream
- 1 tsp. wholegrain mustard

How to make it:

1. Sauté the onion and garlic in butter and olive oil until the onions are soft but not browned. Set aside.
2. Pull the tougher outer leaves off the cabbage and cut around hard inner core. Wash and thinly slice the remaining cabbage.
3. Blanch the shredded cabbage for 2 minutes in boiling water and drain in a colander once boiled.
4. On a medium heat, add the cabbage to the fried onions and garlic in a skillet and heat through for 2 minutes.
5. Add the cream and wholegrain mustard then season with salt and freshly ground black pepper.
6. Serve in separate bowls for a light lunch, or as an accompaniment.

Country Irish Butter Fudge

The Story:

This recipe, a childhood favorite of mine, takes lots of time and patience to make. Almost unique to Northern Ireland, this delicious butter fudge is a country treat and can be found in the kitchens of many an Irish farmhouse where there is the extra time and margin to make such a delicacy. I suppose city folks just don't have the patience, but believe me it's worth the wait. I've made this a part of our *Shamrock & Peach* foods offering and sold it all across the South at various Irish festivals and events and find that folks this side of the Atlantic can't get enough of this country Irish treat. It's crumbly and delicious and not as soft as American fudge tends to be. An instant hit, straight from the Irish farmhouse kitchen!

Butter fudge Ingredients (makes 3½–4 Lbs):

- 10 oz. (1¼ cup) unsalted Irish butter
- 1 large tin (396 g) sweetened condensed milk
- 7 fl. oz. whole milk
- 40 oz. (5 cups) granulated sugar (not fine)

How to make it:

1. Grease a small pan size, approx. 11x7x1.5".
2. In a medium saucepan, combine all the ingredients and slowly bring them to a gentle boil, stirring all the time as the mixture can so easily "catch." (Even if it does at this stage, the caramelized pieces can *still* be beaten and incorporated without sacrificing the quality).
3. When the fudge reaches 236-238 degrees F. on a candy thermometer, begin to stir the fudge constantly on a low and steady boil for the next 35-40 minutes until the fudge reaches the *soft ball* stage. (To test whether the fudge is ready, drop a little mixture into a glass of ice water and it should form a *soft fudge ball* when done).
4. Remove from heat and begin to beat by hand for a further 5–7 minutes or until mixture becomes *fudge-like* in texture.
5. Quickly pour into the prepared pan, scraping down sides of pan so as not to waste any of the creamy goodness.
6. Cool fudge for at least 2 hours before cutting.
7. Store in a dry, airtight container (best not refrigerated).

Farmhouse Sticky Toffee Pudding

The Story:

To many, this recipe is more of a British delight than Irish, but in our farmhouse kitchen this pudding was always a summer treat, served on Sunday evenings with a good cup of tea. In Scotland and Northern Ireland we just love toffee; we include it in many of our dessert dishes, and truly this is one of the best. If you've never tried this before, I strongly recommend giving it a go. As a testament, any of my American friends who have tasted this pudding claim they will never be the same again!

Ingredients for the date purée (makes 10 small puddings):

- 8 oz. (1¾ cups) dates (stoned and chopped)
- 1 tsp. baking soda
- 8 fl. oz. (1 cup) freshly brewed hot coffee

Ingredients for the cake batter:

- 3 oz. butter (softened to room temperature)
- 2 eggs (beaten)
- 6 oz. brown sugar
- 6 oz. (1½ cups) self-rising flour (sifted)
- 2 Tbsp. whole milk
- 1 Tbsp. vanilla

Ingredients for the toffee sauce:

- 7 oz. brown sugar
- 4½ oz. butter
- 4 fl. oz. (½ cup) heavy whipping cream

How to make it:

1. Preheat the oven to 325° F.
2. Grease 10 ramekin dishes.
3. Pour the hot coffee over the roughly chopped dates and baking soda to soften. Purée and set aside.
4. Sift the flour and set aside.
5. Cream the butter and sugar together in an electric mixer until fluffy, then add the beaten eggs one at a time, adding a tablespoon of flour in between.
6. Fold in the remaining flour, using a large metal spoon and alternating with the milk and vanilla. Finally fold in the date purée.
7. Spoon the pudding batter into prepared ramekins. Place on a baking tray and bake for 20–25 minutes.
8. Allow the puddings to rest for 5 minutes and then run a knife around inside each ramekin, turning them out onto a clean, lightly greased baking pan. Cover and set aside.
9. Prepare the toffee sauce by boiling butter, sugar, and cream together for 2 minutes.
10. Poke holes in each cake and pour the warm toffee sauce over pudding.
11. Serve immediately with freshly whipped cream.

Fishing boats at Kilkeel, County Down

Carrick-a-Rede, County Antrim Coast

Newcastle beach, County Down

The Giants Causeway Coast, County Antrim

the Irish coast

Fresh seafood from an island nation, served with centuries of tradition from a people who have learned to live by and love the sea.

The Causeway Coast, County Antrim, Northern Ireland

Kilkeel harbour, County Down

North Antrim Coastline

FRESH LOCAL SEABASS

DOVER SOLE, FRESH BRILL, "PLACE YOUR ORDER"

LOCAL IRISH SALMON ON SALE HERE

Sawers Deli, Belfast, Northern Ireland

The Irish Coast: Wealth From The Sea

Although it is stating the obvious, Ireland is an island, and having a chapter dedicated to the wonders of Irish seafood seemed to be a need I just couldn't ignore. Hemmed in by the mighty Atlantic Ocean on the south and west coasts, the Irish Sea on the east coast, and the cold waters of the North Sea on the north coast, Ireland is a treasure trove of marine goodness. The island also enjoys one of the most dramatic coastlines in the world, with jagged, high cliffs towering above the waves and soft flowing mountains sweeping dramatically down to the beaches while picturesque fishing villages nestle among the cliffs, to the delight of tourists from all over the world. On top of all that, the largest cities on the island, including Dublin, Belfast, Cork, Derry, Waterford, Wexford, and Galway are all coastal towns that gaze out to sea and together account for almost half the population. In fact, no matter where you are on the island, you are never more than an hour from the sea and as a result the culture is distinctly affected by the ocean and the life it brings.

However, as rosy as this picture appears, there is a paradox that exists. Even though Ireland is surrounded by marine wealth, and even though seafood has been a major export for centuries, the Irish people themselves did not seem to embrace the variety of seafood possibilities until fairly recent times. The generations of my parents and grandparents sometimes ate fish, but in quite bland ways; fish that was fried, battered, or set in a pie seemed to be the only alternatives in times past, whereas today the Irish culture has exploded with an incredible range of exciting new restaurants that are specializing in the wonderful seafood that exists right on our doorstep. We have oceanic resources all around us which at last we are using, and in this chapter we will look at that new-found confidence in Irish seafood cuisine.

A few years ago I had my own seafood revival experience in Ireland during a trip with my parents and my husband to Connemara in the west of Ireland. Nestled in the mountains, just a few miles from the sea, we stopped at one of our favorite restaurants to enjoy what turned out to be one of the most amazing culinary experiences of my life. This simple eatery specialized in locally caught seafood and they changed their menu daily to reflect the catch of the fishermen who worked the harbor just ten minutes away. The décor was plain, the menu fairly basic, but the seafood was exquisite. That night I ordered monkfish and haven't been the same since. The dish was prepared in a way that accentuated the natural flavor of the fish without overwhelming it, the accents drew attention to the fish without being overpowering in themselves, and the entire experience was a dish of subtle harmony—just as Irish food should be. As I've said before, the beauty of Irish food is found not so much in the adventurous sauces but in the simplicity of preparation that allows the natural flavors to come through to the fore, letting the quality of the produce speak for itself, and this is certainly how I believe good seafood should be honored, as you will see in the pages that follow.

In this chapter we'll look at several Irish seafood favorites that include fresh and smoked salmon, pan-fried halibut, trout, cod, shrimp, scallops and even a little monkfish as we explore Irish seafood and look at several new ideas for preparing this delicate genre of food. We will give a nod to the past with an old favorite such as battered cod and chips which can be found in most seaside town eateries throughout the island, and fast forward to modern Ireland with some exciting recipes by three of Ireland's most up and coming chefs who I have gotten to know lately and who have been so good to contribute. So, please enjoy our little excursion to the harbors and coves of Ireland as we raise a toast to the wonders of the sea and the Irish coast.

Irish Breakfast Smoked Salmon & Eggs

served on toasted soda farls and garnished with chopped chives

The story:

Eggs are the perfect start to the day and provide one of the best sources of protein to kick-start our metabolism, and this is the perfect dish for a breakfast in bed meal.

I just *love* smoked salmon. It is a low-fat food that I cannot find enough ways to serve, and here is an old traditional Irish seaside recipe that I adapted for my book by adding some cream and chopped chives, serving them on some freshly baked Irish soda bread rounds. As I said, it's the *perfect* special Irish breakfast in bed, paired with a cup of Irish breakfast tea to start your daily routine. Oh, and if you are watching your calories, this meal can easily become a weight watcher's dream. Lighten up the eggs by using half egg whites for whole eggs, change out the heavy whipping cream for skimmed milk, and serve on Irish whole wheat brown bread.

Ingredients (serves 4):

- 1 recipe of Irish Soda Farls baked in rounds (*see "Bakery" chapter*)
- 2 Tbsp. butter (for toast)
- 6 oz. smoked salmon (thinly sliced in thin strips 2" long)
- 3 Tbsp. unsalted butter
- 6 free-range eggs
- salt and white pepper
- 6 Tbsp. heavy cream
- 2 Tbsp. chopped chives

How to make it:

1. Slice smoked salmon in thin strips. Set aside.
2. To make scrambled eggs, gently beat the cream, eggs, salt, and pepper together with a whisk. Heat sauté pan. Add butter and scramble the eggs on medium-low temperature to desired softness. Remove from heat and fold in the chopped smoked salmon.
3. Cut rounds of soda farl in half and place on a grill pan. Toast soda to golden brown. Spread over butter.
4. To assemble, place soda round in the center of plate. Spoon the scrambled egg and smoked salmon on top in a mound. Garnish with chopped chives.
5. Serve right away.

County Down Crab Pate
served on Irish oatcakes with chives and lemon zest

the story:

Crab is an abundant crustacean available on the Irish shores, particularly in County Down fishing harbors, and can be purchased at very reasonable prices. Our most common edible crab is about eight inches wide and a pinkish color, while several other varieties of crab are found in Irish waters, such as the spider crab and the red velvet crab. The majority of the meat is found in the claws of the crab, but with a little bit of extra work the body of the crab also contains some delicious meat which can be used in salads, chowders, soups, pies, crab cakes, and with one of my favorites, this classy little appetizer.

Crab meat is just fantastic served on Irish oatcakes, as the age-old biscuits are nutty and slightly sweet, complementing the crab beautifully. So here I have combined some tangy lump crab meat with cream cheese, crème fraiche, shallots, chives, and horseradish and created these tasty pre-dinner treats. Ready cooked crab meat is available in most fishmongers, but with a little extra work fresh crabs can be boiled whole and the cooked meat removed.

Crab pate Ingredients:

- 8 oz. cream cheese (room temperature)
- 4 fl. oz (½ cup) crème fraiche
- 1 shallot (finely chopped)
- 2 Tbsp. chives (finely chopped)
- ½ tsp. lemon zest
- 1 Tbsp. lemon juice
- 1 Tbsp. milk
- 1 tsp. horseradish sauce
- ¼ tsp. fine sea salt
- freshly ground black pepper
- 8 oz. lump crab meat
- a few chives (to garnish, plus a little lemon zest)
- Irish oatcakes (*see "Irish Bakery" chapter*)

How to make it:

1. Bring the cream cheese to room temperature and then beat to soften with a handheld electric mixer.
2. Gently fold in the crème fraiche, shallot, lemon zest and juice, chives, milk, horseradish, salt, and pepper.
3. Fold in the crab meat using a rubber spatula.
4. Refrigerate for about 2 hours before serving.
5. To serve, place a teaspoon of crab pate on top of a buttered oatcake and add a little lemon zest and ½" piece of chive.

Irish Seafood Chowder
by Chef Wade Murphy

The story:

I had the pleasure of meeting Irish Chef Wade Murphy recently in Atlanta, where we were able to connect and swap some great food ideas, and he graciously agreed to give me this wonderful Irish seafood chowder recipe for *The Shamrock & Peach*. Chowder is in many ways a very American dish, being famous in New England and all along the Eastern seaboard of the United States; but here, Wade has injected a lot of very Irish ingredients into the mix, which I think my American readers will find interesting to work with and also quite unique. Believe me, the results are superb!

Wade is the Executive Head Chef at Doonbeg Golf resort in County Clare and is a rising star in the Irish culinary world; but even with all his culinary success, he does not forget his roots by saying that his best lessons were learned from his grandmother. You have to love that! Thanks, Wade.

Chef Wade Murphy

Ingredients (serves 6):

- 3 medium red potatoes (peeled and cut into ½" dice)
- 1½ pints (3 cups) water
- 3 Tbsp. olive oil
- 1 large onion (finely diced)
- 3 cloves garlic (minced)
- 6 fl. oz. (3/4 cup) dry white wine
- 24 littleneck clams (scrubbed)
- 3 slices of bacon (finely diced)
- 1½ celery rib (finely diced)
- 1½ Tbsp. all-purpose flour
- 12 fl. oz. (1½ cups) heavy cream
- 9 oz. skinless salmon fillet (cut into 1" cubes)
- 9 oz. cleaned monkfish fillet (cut into 1" cubes)
- salt and freshly ground pepper
- 2 Tbsp. chopped parsley

How to make it:

1. In a saucepan, cover the potatoes with the water and bring to a boil. Cover and cook over moderate heat for 6 minutes or until the potatoes are tender. Remove potatoes from the heat and let them stand, covered.
2. Next, in a large saucepan heat 1½ Tbsp. of the oil. Add half of the onion and garlic and cook for 5 minutes over moderate heat until softened. Add the wine and bring to a boil. Add the mussels, cover, and cook.
3. As the clams open, transfer them to the bowl.
4. Strain and reserve the cooking liquid. Remove the mussels and clams from their shells and coarsely chop them.
5. Wipe out the saucepan. Add the remaining 1½ Tbsp. of olive oil and the bacon and cook for 4 minutes over moderate heat until crispy. Add the celery and the remaining onion and garlic. Cover and cook for 7 minutes over moderately low heat until softened. Stir in the flour, then gradually whisk in the potato cooking water.
6. Bring to a boil, whisking, and cook until thickened slightly. Add the potatoes and the cream and bring to a simmer.
7. Add the salmon and monkfish and simmer over moderate heat, stirring for a few minutes until the fish is *just cooked*, which should be about 3 minutes. Add the mussels and clams and pour in their reserved cooking liquid, stopping before you reach the grit at the bottom; stir until heated through.
8. Season with salt and pepper and add the parsley. Serve the chowder in bowls.

Crispy Strangford Rock Oyster & Ardglass Scallop Parcels
with samphire & dipping sauce by Chef Derek Patterson

The story:

When I go home to Northern Ireland, no visit is ever complete without a meal at The Plough Inn in Hillsborough, County Down, the host restaurant of the famous Oyster Festival that takes place in Hillsborough every year, drawing thousands of tourists. Restaurant owner and Chef Derek Patterson tells me that this little recipe is suitable for all types of seafood, such as squid, prawns, monk cheek, sea bass, or shellfish. In this case Derek has chosen some oysters and scallops from Northern Irish shores, which you can replicate at your local fishmongers. Both Strangford and Ardglass are picturesque fishing villages on the County Down coast and are well worth a visit for their beauty as well as their excellent seafood.

Chef Derek Patterson

Seafood ingredients:
- 8 scallops cleaned and roe removed
- 8 rock oysters shucked and cleaned
- 6 oz. blanched and refreshed samphire

Batter ingredients:
- 3½ oz. (100 g) plain flour
- 3½ oz. (100 g) corn flour
- 4 egg whites
- 10½ fl. oz. (300 ml) sparkling water
- pinch of sea salt
- (optional addition of 1 tsp. sesame seeds)

Dipping sauce ingredients:
- 1 Tbsp. sesame oil
- 2 Tbsp. rice wine vinegar
- 2 Tbsp. soy sauce
- 2 Tbsp. miran
- 2 Tbsp. heather honey
- 2 Tbsp. pickled ginger (finely shredded)

How to make it:

1. Heat some peanut oil in your wok or in a deep fat fryer to 375 degrees F. When almost ready, whisk together the ingredients for the batter. (It is best to use the sparkling water chilled and the egg whites from the fridge; the colder the temperature, the crispier the batter.)

2. You may squeeze a little lemon juice over your seafood to give it a citrus twist and sprinkle with a pinch of sea salt, but do not season the samphire, as it tends to be quite salty.

3. Coat the seafood in the light batter, which should have the texture to *barely coat a spoon*. The batter will be golden brown and generally the pieces of seafood will float when ready. The samphire will take the least amount of time, so add it to the fryer last.

4. When removing the seafood and samphire, place on an absorbent piece of kitchen paper and then serve with the dipping sauce.

5. Use unusual serving plates like slate, glass, or driftwood and serve with chopsticks and the dipping sauce.

About the dipping sauce:

1. The dipping sauce is best placed in a small jam jar and shaken vigorously just before serving. Serve in an Asian-style dipping dish so that you can dip your beautiful seafood and coat it generously. The dipping sauce can be stored for a few days in the refrigerator, as it keeps quite well.

Baked Monk fish wrapped in smoked Bacon
with a farmer's market ratatouille

The story:

Monkfish is a common sight at many Irish fish markets and harbors and a very popular choice on menus in restaurants throughout the island. Referred to as "poor man's lobster," as the texture and flavor is quite reminiscent of the fabled crustacean, it's actually a very versatile fish to cook with.

When working with monkfish, we only eat the tail of the fish, which is firm, white meat and in this recipe is able to carry the flavors of the bacon and thyme very nicely. Monkfish is widely available in the United States and I urge you to give it a try; serve with a colorful and rich Southern style ratatouille, and this combination is a winner!

Baked monkfish ingredients:

- 8 slices of uncured thinly sliced smoked bacon
- 4 (5 oz.) pieces of monkfish tail (boneless)
- ground black pepper
- zest of one lemon
- 2 Tbsp. unsalted butter
- 1 Tbsp. vegetable oil
- thyme sprig (to garnish)

Farmers market ratatouille ingredients:

- 3 Tbsp. olive oil
- 1 small onion (chopped)
- 2 cloves garlic (crushed)
- 1 red pepper (seeded and chopped)
- 1 yellow pepper (seeded and chopped)
- 1 ear of fresh corn
- 1 small eggplant
- handful of okra (ends removed and chopped)
- 1 medium zucchini (thinly sliced)
- one 14 oz. can organic chopped plum tomatoes
- 1 Tbsp. fresh thyme (chopped)
- coarse salt and pepper

How to make it:

1. Preheat your oven to 400° F.
2. Season the monkfish with a little ground black pepper and zest of lemon.
3. Lay two slices of bacon out flat and wrap around the outside of each of the fillets.
4. Melt 2 Tbsp. butter and 1 Tbsp. oil on medium-high in skillet and sear the monkfish fillets for 1 minute on each side.
5. Place the skillet in the oven and bake for about 8–10 minutes or until fish is flaky and the bacon is crispy.
6. Remove the monkfish from the oven.
7. To serve, place a large spoonful of ratatouille in the center of the plate and set the monkfish on top in the center. Garnish with a sprig of thyme.

How to make Southern style ratatouille:

1. Heat some olive oil in a large sauté pot.
2. Begin by cooking the onions and garlic until they are soft and then add yellow peppers and cook for 2 minutes to soften.
3. Next, add the egg plant, okra, and corn and cook for a few more minutes.
4. Finish with the zucchini and stir for 1 minute.
5. Add the tomatoes and simmer for 5 more minutes.
6. Stir in thyme and season with salt and pepper.

Seared Scallops with Date Jam and Curried Cauliflower Purée
with Date Jam and Curried Cauliflower Purée

Chef Neven Maguire

The story:

Chef Neven Maguire is a culinary star in Ireland and beyond, and has provided me with this incredible dish which adds elegance with sophistication. Its success lies in the perfect combination of three components: the sweetness of the scallops and the fragrance of the cauliflower purée with the slight taste of toffee from the date jam. Altogether a wonderful dish!

Scallops and date jam ingredients (serves 6):
- 18 large sea scallops, well trimmed
- olive oil, for cooking

For the date jam:
- 8 oz. (1¾ cups) Medjool dates, pitted
- 2 Tbsp. crème de cassis
- 2 tsp. balsamic vinegar
- 2 Tbsp. light muscovado sugar

For the cauliflower purée:
- 1 small cauliflower
- 1 oz. butter
- 1 tsp. mild curry powder
- 2 Tbsp. milk
- 3½ fl. oz. cream
- Maldon sea salt and freshly ground black pepper
- about 6 Tbsp. five-spice balsamic cream, to garnish

Five-spice balsamic cream ingredients:
- 5 fl. oz. heavy whipping cream
- 5 fl. oz. beef stock
- 1 tsp. Chinese five-spice powder
- 1 Tbsp. tomato purée
- 2 Tbsp. balsamic vinegar
- salt and freshly ground black pepper

How to make Five-spice balsamic cream:
1. Place the cream in a saucepan with the stock, five spice, tomato purée, and balsamic vinegar. Bring to a boil, then reduce the heat and simmer for about 5 minutes until reduced and thickened. Season to taste and keep warm or leave to cool completely, then transfer to a bowl and cover with plastic wrap. This can be stored in the fridge for up to three days and reheated as needed.

How to make it:
1. To make the date jam, place 300 ml (½ pint) of water in a pan with the dates. Bring to a simmer and cook gently for 10–15 minutes until the dates are completely soft and the liquid is slightly reduced. Stir in the crème de cassis, vinegar, and sugar and cook for another minute or so until the sugar has dissolved. Leave to cool, then blend in food processor until smooth. Transfer to a bowl and cover with plastic wrap until needed.
2. To make the cauliflower purée, trim the cauliflower into small florets, discarding the leaves and tough stalk. Melt the butter in a pan with a lid and stir in the curry powder. Add the florets and cook for 3 minutes until just beginning to soften, stirring regularly. Add milk and cream, cover, and simmer for another 8 minutes or until the cauliflower is completely soft and the milk mixture is slightly reduced. Place in a food processor or use a hand blender and whisk to a smooth purée. Pass through a sieve into a bowl. Season to taste and either leave to cool completely and cover with plastic wrap in the fridge until needed or, if using immediately, keep warm.
3. To cook the scallops, heat a teaspoon of the oil in a non-stick frying pan. Quickly season the scallops with some salt, then quickly sear scallops for about 1 minute on each side until golden brown and nicely caramelized. They should still be slightly undercooked in the middle. You may need to do this in batches depending on the size of your pan.
4. Warm the five-spice balsamic cream in a small pan. Spoon a little of the cauliflower purée onto each warmed plate and arrange three scallops on each one. Add a spoonful of the date jam and then drizzle around a little of the five-spice balsamic cream to serve.

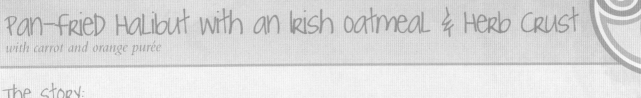

Pan-Fried Halibut with an Irish Oatmeal & Herb Crust
with carrot and orange purée

The Story:

I love the simplicity and purity of this dish because it incorporates Irish rolled oats, which is one of Ireland's great traditional foods, and brings texture and flavor to the fish without overpowering it. The carrot and orange purée is wonderfully light and refreshing and adds a wonderful streak of color to the plate as well as a delicious kick to the overall flavor of the dish.

Oats are a great source of Omega 3 and present an easy way to introduce whole grains to family meals with crispy oat goodness.

Halibut and oatmeal crust ingredients:

- 4 halibut fillets (6 oz. each)
- 4½ oz. (¾ cups) Irish rolled oats
- 1 oz. (¼ cup) all-purpose flour
- 1 tsp. salt
- ¼ tsp. ground black pepper
- 2 tsp. tarragon (chopped) plus little extra to garnish
- 2 eggs (beaten)
- 2 Tbsp. buttermilk
- oil for frying
- orange zest (to garnish)

Carrot and orange purée ingredients:

- 6 medium carrots or 1 lb. (peeled and cut)
- 2 fluid oz. (¼ cup) heavy whipping cream
- 2 fluid oz. (¼ cup) chicken stock
- juice of 1 medium orange (1/3 cup)
- ½ tsp. salt
- ¼ tsp. pepper

How to make it:

1. Rinse the fish fillets and pat dry with paper towels.
2. Measure the oats, flour, salt, pepper, and tarragon out and pulse everything together in the food processor for a few seconds until it is the consistency of corn meal.
3. Prepare carrot purée by filling a medium saucepan with cold water and bring the carrots to a boil. Cook carrots for 10–12 minutes or until tender when pierced with a fork.
4. Drain the carrots in a colander then blend the carrots in a food processor or blender with chicken stock, orange juice, and cream. Add salt and pepper and taste to adjust seasoning.
5. Beat the buttermilk and eggs together in a shallow bowl.
6. Add oil to a deep-sided skillet and bring to medium-high heat.
7. Dip the fish in the oatmeal mixture and then in the eggs and buttermilk. Double dip the fish in the oatmeal.
8. Place fish into the hot oil and cook for about 5–6 minutes, turning once. The batter should be golden and crispy and the fish, flaky and white.
9. 9. To serve, place purée in center of plate and then add the oat-crusted fish on top. Sprinkle with a little fresh tarragon and orange zest.

Irish Salmon wrapped in Pastry Parcels
with a lemon & dill sauce and carrot & leek julienne

The Story:

Fresh fish wrapped in pastry is a French cuisine concept, I concede, but I have taken the *en croûte* idea in this recipe and given it a Celtic spin with Irish/Scottish salmon and the pairing of carrot and leek inside the pastry parcel. To top it off I've created a sauce pairing of lemon with dill, which complements all the flavors and creates *just* enough sweetness and tanginess to lift this dish to another level. Altogether quite a sophisticated dish to serve to guests and pretty easy to make!

Salmon in pastry ingredients (serves 4):

- 4 salmon fillets (2–3 oz.)
- 1 tsp. coarse smoked sea salt
- 3 Tbsp. butter
- 2 carrots (¾ cup) (julienne)
- 1 large leek (¾ cup) (julienne)
- 1 tsp. fresh dill
- ¼ tsp. salt
- pinch of pepper
- 1 egg (beaten)
- 1 Tbsp. water
- 1 sheet from a (17.3 oz.) package frozen puff pastry (thawed)
- 2 Tbsp. flour
- 4 sprigs of fresh dill (garnish)

Lemon dill sauce ingredients:

- 8 fl. oz. (1 cup) dry white wine (Chardonnay)
- 2 tsp. lemon juice
- 8 fl. oz. (1 cup) heavy cream
- 1 tsp. salt
- 1/8 tsp. ground white pepper
- 1 Tbsp. fresh dill

How to make it:

1. In a skillet, sauté the julienne leeks and carrots for about 2 ½–3 minutes until they're just beginning to soften. Season with salt and pepper and set aside to cool.
2. Preheat the oven to 400° F.
3. Line a baking sheet with parchment paper and lightly grease the paper.
4. In a small bowl mix together the egg and water wash.
5. On a lightly floured surface, use a rolling pin to roll out one sheet of the puff pastry to around 1/8" thickness, then divide the pastry into four squares.
6. Season the salmon with a little of the aromatic savory salts.
7. Spoon a tablespoon of the sautéed leeks into the center of each pastry square and add a sprinkle of chopped dill. Complete the filling by placing the salmon on top, cutting the salmon to fit nicely.
8. Brush the edges of the pastry with a little of the egg wash, then fold to form a parcel around the contents and press with a fork to seal. Cut a few small slits in the top of each parcel with a sharp knife.
9. Transfer the salmon with the seam side down to prepared baking dish. Brush the top of each pastry parcel with the egg wash and bake until golden brown for 15–20 minutes.
10. Prepare the lemon dill sauce by combining the wine and lemon juice in a small saucepan. Bring the mixture to a boil and simmer until it has been reduced by ¾. Add the cream and continue to cook until the sauce has been reduced by half. Stir in the dill and add salt and pepper.
11. To serve, cut the salmon parcels in half at a diagonal. Drizzle with the lemon dill sauce and garnish with a piece of fresh dill with stem.

Sparkling Seaside Battered Fish and Chips

with malt vinegar and fresh tartar sauce

The Story:

Seafood has always been good in Ireland because, as an island nation in the north Atlantic, we have been surrounded by the wealth of the oceans for millennia. However, despite this richness, the favorite seafood dish for Irish people in my parents' and grandparents' generation has been the humble Fish and Chip. The local fish and chip shop was a feature of every village in Ireland, and I can still remember the smell of malt vinegar that seemed to fill the air and waft out the chip shop door on cold damp nights. In Northern Ireland this dish is locally known as a "Fish supper" and is usually made with cod or another flaky white fish. Serve with mushy peas and a wedge of lemon for that Irish seaside experience!

Battered fish & chips ingredients (serves 4):

- vegetable oil for deep fat frying
- 3 large russet potatoes
- 1½ lbs. of flaky white fish such as cod or haddock
- malt vinegar and salt (to serve)

Sparkling spring water batter ingredients:

- 1 egg yolk
- 2 oz. (½ cup) cornstarch
- 2 oz. (½ cup) plain flour
- 8 fl. oz. (1 cup) very cold sparkling spring water
- 1 tsp. salt
- ¼ tsp. white pepper

Tartar sauce ingredients:

- 8 fl. oz. (1 cup) mayo
- 1 tsp. yellow mustard
- 1 Tbsp. capers (chopped)
- 1 Tbsp. lemon juice (plus a little lemon zest)
- 1 Tbsp. tarragon (chopped)
- pinch of salt and pepper

How to make it:

1. First, prepare tartar sauce ahead of time by mixing all the ingredients together and refrigerate until ready to serve.
2. Next, heat 2–3" of oil in heavy saucepan or use a deep fat fryer heated to 325° F.
3. Peel the potatoes, slice lengthwise, and slice into large chips or potato wedges, as they are known in America.
4. Fry the potatoes for about 3 minutes in the oil until they are soft but not brown. Drain over paper towels.
5. In a small bowl, mix together the egg yolk and very cold sparkling water using a whisk. Measure out the flour, corn flour, salt, and pepper and add a little at a time to water and egg mixture, being careful not to over-mix.
6. Dip the fish into the batter.
7. Switch temperature of your fryer up to 350° to medium-high.
8. Fry the fish for 2 minutes on each side until golden brown and crispy. Remove and drain over paper towels.
9. Place the chips back in the deep fat fryer or heavy saucepan. Fry the chips for 4–5 minutes until golden brown.
10. Serve right away sprinkled with malt vinegar and plenty of sea salt.

Irish baked scones

the Irish Bakery

The delightful aroma of freshly baked bread creates a wonderful sense of home, a warm welcome to visitors and a smile to everyone's face.

Field of Barley on our farm at Gilford, County Armagh

Hillsborough, County Down

Tea Room & Bakery, County Down

Dad McLoughlin hard at work

An Irish Soda Bannock, fresh from the oven

The Irish Bakery: An Age-Old Craft

When visitors return from Ireland, they have a tendency to mention several distinctive things about the Irish country and culture that will stay with them as memories, and these delights keep coming up over and over again—the intense green of the landscape, the beauty of the cliffs and the mountains, the warmth of the Irish people, the renowned Irish breakfast, the famous Irish pint, or the wonderful Irish breads. Served on the breakfast table, in tea rooms, at coffee houses, and in wee little bakeries that dot the landscape, the distinctive breads of Ireland are a talking point for visitors and a source of longing for Irish immigrants who can't quite seem to recreate those wonderful breads in their new host country. They remember the griddle breads, such as potato farls or soda bread or wheaten farls or delicious oatmeal scones with salty butter, and they smile at the memory.

Irish breads are fairly distinctive because of how the Irish people lived and cooked for centuries on the island, separated from the rest of Europe. Ireland, for example, has no real history of yeast in bread making. Typically, Irish cooks made extensive use of the iron griddle perched over a fire, as historically Irish people did not use or construct ovens. The open fire was the center of the home, as it is in country farmhouses today, burning aromatic turf, the smoke of which just added to the flavors of the foods they cooked. They used ingredients that were easily available in the Irish countryside, with buttermilk and soda acting as the leavening agents in place of yeast and giving their breads that distinct flavor. In Ireland, in fact, baking with yeast was traditionally viewed with much suspicion by Irish cooks, who regarded yeast cookery as a lengthy and arduous process in comparison. This has changed today, of course, with modern Irish bakers taking on other styles of bread making from many cultures of the world, both in the home and in restaurants, but the culture of Irish griddle bread, I'm happy to say, is still alive and well in country kitchens throughout the land.

In this chapter we will explore some of those delightful breads that have gained such notoriety and have helped to keep those visitors to Ireland rolling in. We'll make griddle delights and favorites such as soda bread, delicious scones, wheaten, and potato bread. These are the staples that Irish families enjoy day in and day out with preserves and butter or in a fry with bacon, eggs, and mushrooms. Their uses are varied, but the results are always the same, as I have found out in my own food business here in Atlanta. People just love these distinctive Irish breads.

My father-in-law, Jimmy McLoughlin, who worked in one of Northern Ireland's largest bakeries for fifty years in County Armagh, has in the last number of years taught me many of the skills that have increased my love of baking and bread making. He passed on to me the secrets of making these truly Irish breads and I hope in some way this chapter and this book keep those traditions alive as Ireland becomes increasingly cosmopolitan.

As you will discover, in Irish bread making there is something therapeutic and tactile about kneading the dough to the right consistency, which is almost an art form in itself, while using *just* the right amount of flour—too much, and the bread will not bake properly as it has been overworked, too little, and the consistency will be too sticky and premature to form the texture we love in well-made breads. This takes practice and patience, but stick with it and you will be rewarded with those wonderful smells that fill the home as the breads brown in the oven. No wonder homes are sold using those aromas, as we enjoy the wonders of baking.

So please enjoy these pages and these recipes that were crafted with such love and care as you carry on the tradition of Irish bread making in the warmth and comfort of your own kitchen.

Irish Country Soda Bread Bannock and Farls

The Story:

Irish soda bread is a quick bread traditionally made on a cast iron griddle over an open fire, using what appear to be quite odd ingredients. There is no yeast in soda bread, with the leavening agent instead being a combination of bicarbonate soda and buttermilk. Both of these ingredients, when combined in the baking process, create carbon dioxide gas that in turn causes the bread to rise in the oven. The result is a uniquely delicious and light bread that works perfectly with a wide range of other foods and toppings. The loaf is typically rolled into a circle called a "bannock" and cut into four triangles, which are called "farls" in Northern Ireland. The farls, though, as you can see below, may also be made separately on a griddle.

Soda bread bannock ingredients:

- 1 lb. (4 cups) plain flour (sifted)
- ½ tsp. salt
- 1 tsp. baking soda (sifted)
- 1 Tbsp. sugar
- 16 fl. oz. (2 cups) buttermilk
- 1 egg (beaten)
- 1 Tbsp. Irish butter (melted)

Soda Farls (Ulster griddle cooked flatbread) ingredients:

- 8 oz. (2 cups) plain flour
- ¼ tsp. salt
- ½ tsp. baking soda (sift)
- 1 Tbsp. shortening
- 8 fl. oz. (1 cup) buttermilk

How to make Soda bread:

1. Measure all the dry ingredients together and sift to incorporate as much air as possible.
2. Make a well in the center of the flour and add enough buttermilk, beaten egg, and melted butter to get an easily handled soft dough.
3. Knead very lightly and form into a circle then make a cross in the center using a knife.
4. Bake at 425° F for 40–45 minutes.
5. To test, gently tap bottom of bannock (bread is ready when it sounds hollow).

How to make Soda Farls:

6. To make the farls, preheat a griddle to medium-high heat.
7. Measure dry ingredients and sift. Rub in the shortening, add the buttermilk, and bind together with large metal spoon.
8. Knead very lightly with floured hands, then use a floured rolling pin to roll the dough into a circle 4" in diameter. Cut into quarters with a floured sharp knife.
9. Place each quarter on a hot griddle and cook for about 10–12 minutes on each side. (Cover farls with a clean, dry tea towel when cooking on the griddle).
10. Farls are ready when bread is golden brown and the sides are firm to the touch.

Irish Wheaten Bread
also known as Brown Soda Bread

The Story:

My friend Myrtle is famous in County Armagh for her Wheaten Bread (or brown soda bread) and she has kindly shared her recipe for my cookbook. It is full of fiber, yeast-free, and so simple to prepare. Delicious with a salad for High tea, toasted for breakfast, or as the base for an elegant appetizer. If you are able to pick up some Irish imported brown whole wheat flour, you will get the best results.

Ingredients (makes 3 loaves in a 1-lb. tin):

- 1 lb. (3 cups) coarse whole wheat flour
- 5 oz. (1¼ cup) flour
- 5 oz. (1¼ cup) oats
- 1 tsp. salt
- 3 tsp. baking soda
- 2 oz. (½ cup) wheat germ
- 3 oz. sugar (3/8 cup)
- 3 oz. butter or margarine
- 1 egg (beaten)
- 1½ pints (3 cups) buttermilk
- 1 Tbsp. honey

How to make it:

1. Preheat oven to 425° F. Grease and flour 3 small 8x4x2" loaf pans.
2. Measure all the dry ingredients in a large bowl. Rub in the butter you're your fingertips and create a well in the center of the mix.
3. Beat the eggs in a small bowl and mix with the buttermilk and honey. Add to the dry ingredients and mix well with a large spoon.
4. Transfer the resulting dough to a floured surface and knead gently with floured hands.
5. Divide the dough into loaves and place each loaf into prepared tins. Using a knife, cut a line down center of each loaf.
6. Bake for 40 minutes until a deep golden brown color or until base of loaf sounds hollow when lightly tapped.

McNeill Family Irish Oatcakes

The Story:

My great-great-grandfather claimed on his 100th birthday that these crunchy little bites are the secret to extending long life, and so listed here is the McNeill family recipe which I hope will do the same for you!

The Irish have been making these for millennia, cooked on a hot griddle over an open fire using locally grown oats, and to illustrate their longevity, a high cross in Moone, County Kildare, carved in the tenth century, even depicts the parable of the five loaves and two fishes from the Gospels as three oatcakes and two eels! So, they were deemed good enough for a miracle! These versatile bites can be served with cheese or pate as an elegant appetizer or simply eaten with butter and preserves.

Ingredients (makes 12 oatcakes):

- 8 oz. (1 cup) steal cut oatmeal
- 1 ½ oz. (3/8 cup) all purpose flour
- 1/8 tsp. baking soda
- ½ tsp. salt
- 3 Tbsp. butter (melted)
- 3–4 Tbsp. boiling water
- 2 Tbsp. sugar
- flour and oatmeal (to roll out)

How to make them:

1. Preheat a griddle to a moderate heat or your oven to 325° F.
2. Combine the oats, all purpose white flour, baking soda, sugar, and salt, making a well in the center of the dry ingredients with a large metal spoon.
3. Pour boiling water over the butter to melt then combine with the dry ingredients and mix to make a dough.
4. Sprinkle the surface with some flour and oats.
5. Roll the dough out in a circle ¼" thick, incorporating extra oats and flour to prevent sticking.
6. Use a small 1 ½" cookie cutter to form 12 oatcakes or cut with a knife into triangles.
7. Transfer to a lightly greased cookie sheet.
8. Transfer oatcakes to griddle and bake for 12–15 minutes on each side until hard and crisp. Alternatively, bake the oatcakes in oven for 30 minutes until golden brown.
9. Leave them in the oven with the *light on* to dry out overnight for a crisp oatcake. Cool on a wire wrack.
10. Store in an airtight container.
11. Best served buttered with Irish cheese or with the *Crab Pate recipe* featured in the *Irish Coast* chapter.

Oatcakes and eels carved in the ancient high cross in Moone, County Kildare

famous OLD fashioned Potato Bread farls

the story:

This much-loved and quintessentially Irish griddle bread has been adapted into many variations within Ireland, each one unique to its region of the island. The primary recipe listed here is the general northern version, which is common throughout bakeries in Ulster. Used in the great *Ulster Fry* primarily, it is very much a popular bread throughout Northern Ireland. *Boxty*, on the other hand, is regional only to the northwest area of Ireland in Counties Fermanagh and Derry, while *Pratie Oaten* is regional purely to the northeast, the area of Northern Ireland that overlooks Scotland.

I suggest that you try out all these wonderful variations and see which one you like best! I also suggest that in making this bread you use a floury variety of potato (Russet or Idaho) for best results.

Ulster Potato Bread ingredients:

- 1 lb. (2 cups) cooked mashed potatoes
- 1 tsp. salt
- 2 Tbsp. butter (melted)
- 4–6 oz (1–1½ cups) all purpose flour
- little flour (to coat working and cooking surface)

HOW TO MAKE THE VARIATIONS:

Spring Onion Potato Bread (delicious with Ulster Fry)

- Add 2 spring onions (green parts only) finely chopped to the dough before cooking.

Apple Potato Bread

- 2 medium-sized tart apples (peeled and sliced) plus 3 Tbsp. water

1. Combine the apples and water in a small saucepan and cook on medium for 8–10 minutes to soften.
2. Drain the apples. Cool and chop a little with a knife before adding to potatoes.

Cheese Potato Bread (I suggest this with BLT Appetizer Bites)

- Add 2 oz. grated Irish cheddar cheese to the dough before cooking.

Pratie Oaten (famous in North Coast of Northern Ireland)

- Replace the flour with pinhead oats

Old-Fashioned Boxty (famous in Northwest of Ireland)

- Replace 1 cup of the cooked mashed potatoes with 1 cup of grated raw potato

How to make it (makes 16 triangles):

1. Cut the potatoes into small pieces and place in a small, heavy-based saucepan half-filled with cold water.
2. Boil for 15–20 minutes, drain well, and allow potatoes to dry out before mashing.
3. Add the salt and melted butter and as much flour as the potatoes will absorb.
4. Turn onto a lightly floured surface and knead lightly so that all the flour is combined (the amount of flour can often be a little less depending on variety of potato).
5. Cut the dough into four triangles with a knife.
6. Use a lightly floured rolling pin to roll each ball of dough into a ¼" thick circle.
7. Cut into 4 triangles again to make 16 pieces.
8. Preheat griddle to moderate heat. Lightly flour surface.
9. Cook the bread for 3 minutes per side or until they are golden brown.

Apple and Flax Morning Glory Muffins

with oats, flax, apple, raisins, and carrots

The story:

The blue flax flower is the symbol of the new Northern Ireland, adorning all the literature pertaining to the Northern Ireland Assembly and even adorning our very own Ulster Kitchen logo, among other things! Reason being that the flax plant put Ulster on the map in days gone by as linen production hurled the north of Ireland into the industrial revolution and in many ways created the cultural legacy we have today. In addition to this, flax seeds are also *really* good for you, being rich in Omega 3 fats, fiber, and antioxidants. Then, when combined into a morning food that packs a wonderful nutritional punch, these muffins are sure to be a winner, coming in really handy if you need to make breakfast on the fly!

Muffin ingredients (makes 12–14):

- 5 oz. (1 ¼ cup) all-purpose flour
- 2 ½ oz. (¼ cup) whole wheat flour
- 1 Tbsp. baking powder
- 1 tsp. cinnamon
- ½ tsp. ginger
- ½ tsp. salt
- 6 Tbsp. old-fashioned rolled oats
- 4 Tbsp. flax seed flour
- 4 oz. (½ cup) light brown sugar
- 1 large egg (beaten)
- 8 fl. oz. (1 cup) buttermilk
- 2 2/3 fl. oz. (1/3 cup) walnut oil
- 1 Tbsp. vanilla
- 2 medium-sized carrots (scraped and grated)
- 2 medium-sized apples (peeled and grated)
- 3 oz. (½ cup) raisins
- 2 oz. (½ cup) walnuts (chopped)

Muffin topping ingredients:

- 2 oz. (½ cup) walnuts (chopped)
- 1 Tbsp. flax seed flour
- 1 Tbsp. oats

How to make them:

1. Preheat your oven to 375° F.
2. Grease or line muffin pans or use muffin paper liners.
3. Sift both of the flours, the baking powder, salt, cinnamon, and ginger in a mixing bowl. Add the oats, flax seed flour, and brown sugar.
4. In a separate bowl, beat the egg and mix in the buttermilk, oil, and vanilla. Add the grated carrots, apples, and raisins.
5. Combine the wet mixture with the dry flour mixture, gently stirring to combine.
6. Divide the muffin batter evenly between the muffin pans and fill each cup 2/3 full.
7. Sprinkle the tops of each muffin with walnuts, flax seed flour, and oats.
8. Bake for 20–25 minutes.
9. Remove the muffins from pan and cool on a rack.

Ulster Kitchen Signature Butter Shortbread

The Story:

During the Christmas holidays I cannot keep up with the demand for these crunchy, crumbly cookies. Famous in Scotland, shortbread is also a staple and classic cookie in Northern Ireland and they are absolutely perfect with a cup of Irish breakfast tea! I love to dip them in creamy Cranachan or Irish Tipsy Trifle and they make a perfect dinner party ending. For added fun, try cutting them with Shamrock cookie cutters for St. Patrick's Day celebrations!

Ingredients:

- 1 cup (8 oz.) butter
- 4 oz. (3/4 cup) powdered sugar
- 8 oz. (2 cups) all purpose flour
- 1 oz. (1/4 cup) cornstarch
- 1 oz. (1/4 cup) rice flour
- 3 Tbsp. granulated sugar (to sprinkle over baked cookies)

How to make them:

1. Preheat oven to 325° F.
2. Cream the butter and sugar together until light and fluffy in an electric mixer.
3. Measure the flour, cornstarch, and rice flour together then slowly incorporate the dry ingredients into the creamed butter and sugar. Mix until fully incorporated.
4. Place the resulting shortbread dough onto a floured surface and use a lightly floured rolling pin to roll out the dough to ¼" thick.
5. Cut into desired shape with a suitable cookie cutter and place on baking sheets.
6. Bake for 12 minutes until the edges of the cookies are a light golden brown.
7. Sprinkle with sugar while still warm and leave to cool in the pan for about 5 minutes before transferring to a wire rack to cool completely.
8. Store in an airtight container.

Classic Irish Oatmeal Cookies

The Story:

I have memories of these cookies, or *biscuits* as they're known of in Northern Ireland, being freshly baked and arranged on cooling racks in my grandmother's kitchen and always flavored with her love. An Irish tradition, these crunchy cookies, flavored with old-fashioned oats, work well with many toppings and in many variations, some of which I have included here. Delicious with tea and coffee, these cookies will fill your kitchen with a wonderful aroma during baking that will transport you back to Ireland itself.

Ingredients (makes 2½ dozen cookies):

- 8 oz. (1 cup) unsalted butter
- 4 oz. (½ cup) soft light brown sugar
- 4 oz. (½ cup) all-purpose flour
- ½ tsp. baking soda
- 3 oz. (3/8 cup) coconut (use unsweetened, organic dried)
- 9 oz. (2.83 cups) old-fashioned oats
- Pinch salt

VARIATIONS:

Chocolate Pecan Oatmeal Cookies Ingredients:

- 2 oz. (1/3 cup) quality milk chocolate
- 1 oz (1/4 cup) toasted chopped pecans

1. Using a teaspoon place a small amount of melted chocolate in center of cookie. Sprinkle with toasted pecans.

Coffee Butter Cream topping (with toasted walnuts) Ingredients:

- 4 oz (½ cup) butter
- 6 oz (1 ½ cups) powdered sugar
- ½ tsp. coffee essence (or instant coffee dissolved in a little boiling water)
- toasted walnut halves

1. Prepare the icing by creaming together the butter, powdered sugar and coffee essence together until light and fluffy.
2. Spoon the butter cream into a piping bag and, using a star-shaped nozzle, pipe a small knob of icing onto the center of each cookie and garnish with a toasted walnut.

How to make them:

1. Preheat the oven to 325° F.
2. Measure and combine the flour, baking soda, oatmeal, salt and coconut together.
3. Cream the butter and sugar in a bowl and beat until they are light and fluffy.
4. Add the remaining ingredients and mix until they are fully incorporated.
5. Refrigerate for at least 15 minutes to allow the dough to become firm.
6. Lightly flour a surface and roll out the dough to a thickness of about ½" using a floured rolling pin.
7. Press mixture down with floured hands to form a circle, then use your rolling pin to level the dough to about 1/3" thick.
8. Cut out the cookies using a 1½"-round cookie cutter and place on a cookie sheet.
9. Bake for 12–15 minutes until the cookies are a light golden color. Dip the top of warm cookies in a shallow bowl of fine granulated sugar and set on wire rack to cool.

The OLD Irish Earl Tea Bread

The Story:

Technically speaking, Charles Grey, the Earl synonymous with the flavorful tea, was not Irish, but he married a lady from an Irish background, and was a great friend of Daniel O'Connell, and his son was Lord Lieutenant of Ireland, so we're claiming him! Seriously though, I just love tea bread made with Earl Grey tea, as the flavors permeate the bread to create a delicious aroma and complementary flavor when served with afternoon tea, so in terms of flavor, you get the whole teatime package.

Tea breads may be baked with differing flavors of tea, but I just prefer the dear old Earl whose tea derives its flavor from oil of Bergamot, an Italian-grown acidic orange. So give this a try and toast the dear old Irish Earl!

Ingredients:

- 12 oz. (2 cups) mixed dried fruit (dried cherries, cranberries, blueberries)
- 4 oz. (½ cup) glaze cherries (chopped)
- 8 fl. oz. (1 cup) cold Earl Grey tea
- 1 tsp. vanilla
- 8 oz. (2 cups) self-rising flour
- ½ tsp. cinnamon
- ¼ tsp. nutmeg
- grated rind of one orange
- 4 oz. (½ cup) brown sugar
- 1 egg (lightly beaten)
- wax paper (to line tin)

How to make it:

1. Place the mixed fruit, chopped cherries, and sugar in a bowl and pour over the cold tea and vanilla.
2. Cover and soak overnight.
3. Preheat your oven to 350° F.
4. Line a standard 8x4x2½" loaf pan with wax paper.
5. Add the beaten egg and flour to the soaked mixture then mix well.
6. Pour into a prepared loaf pan and bake for 45 minutes (test with skewer; you will know when the skewer comes out clean).
7. Serve buttered with a cup of tea.

VARIATIONS OF TEA BREAD

Irish Whiskey Bread
- Substitute whiskey for half of the tea

Irish Stout Bread
- Substitute Irish Stout for the tea

Raspberry & White Chocolate Buttermilk Scones
with raspberry freezer jam

The Story:

These wonderful scones are the result of years of perfecting the most delicious teatime scone possible. Each year I cater scores of tea parties as part of my food business, The Ulster Kitchen, and these Irish scones are the number one favorite item, so, I just had to include them in my Irish Bakery all-star list! The light, buttermilk texture of the scones works wonders with the white chocolate, accented with raspberries. Also, if you prefer, you can switch out the raspberries for blueberries for a different accent.

Top with some raspberry preserve, a dollop of fresh cream, serve with some Irish breakfast tea, and you'll have a winning combination.

Buttermilk Scone ingredients (makes 12–15 scones):
- 1 lb. (4 cups) self-rising flour
- 1 tsp. baking powder
- 4 oz. (½ cup) sugar
- 6 oz. (¾ cup) butter
- 2 eggs (beaten)
- 6 fl. oz. (¾ cup) buttermilk
- handful of white chocolate chips (plus extra to drizzle)
- handful of dried or fresh frozen raspberries
- 1 egg beaten with 1 Tbsp. of water (to glaze)

Easy Raspberry Freezer Jam Ingredients:
- 1 ½ lbs. red raspberries (crushed)
- 2 ¼ lbs. fine granulated sugar
- 4 fl. oz. (½ cup) liquid pectin

How to make it:
1. Crush the raspberries and stir in the sugar.
2. Refrigerate overnight, stirring occasionally.
3. Add the pectin and stir the fruit mixture until fully incorporated.
4. Pour jam into clean, sterilized glass jars or plastic containers. Allow jam to set for a day at room temperature before freezing for up to 1 year.

How to make them:
1. Preheat the oven to 425° F.
2. Sift together the flour, sugar, and baking powder in a bowl.
3. Rub the butter into the mixture with your fingers until it resembles coarse crumbs.
4. Make a well in the center of dry mixture then set aside.
5. In another bowl, combine the egg and buttermilk then fold all at once into the dry mixture.
6. Stir until moistened then knead 4 or 5 times to create the dough.
7. Using your knuckles, create a large pocket in the center of the dough, filling it with the raspberries and white chocolate chips. Gently knead to combine.
8. Use a floured rolling pin to flatten the dough to measure about 1" in height.
9. Cut scones using a 1 ½" fluted pastry or cookie cutter, and place each cutout on a large baking pan. Brush the tops with egg glaze using a pastry brush.
10. Bake for 15 minutes until the scones are a light golden brown, turning the pan around halfway through baking time to ensure evenness.
11. Allow to cool then drizzle with a little melted white chocolate over the scones.

The welcome of American shores

The road ahead that led from Northern Ireland to the Deep South

Coming to America

Southern hospitality with an Irish twist. A three hundred year old tale of two cultures that share a love of story and food

Dogwoods in bloom, Marietta, Georgia

Carrick-a-rede ropebridge, County Antrim

Covered bridge, Roswell Georgia

Leaving Northern Ireland, coming to America

The legacy of three hundred years of transatlantic immigration manifests itself today in a fascination and counter-fascination between Ireland and America. In Ireland, many people dream of coming to America, of seeing the great landscapes, the cities, the skyscrapers, and the fast-paced culture. In America, people in turn dream of going to mystical Ireland. They long to see the green mountains, to walk the narrow lanes, to sleep in a castle, and of course to eat the wonderful Irish food from the land. Such are the ties between our two nations, but why is this so?

Scots-Irish immigration to the Americas began three hundred years ago, before the countries of Ireland and America came to exist as sovereign nations. Both were colonies of Great Britain and both were in a constant state of flux with immigrants reshaping their respective ancient cultures. In the North of Ireland, Scots immigrants, or *planters* as they were known, had arrived in thousands from lowland Scotland in a land grab sanctioned by James I. They were hardworking, deeply religious people, but after several decades the plantation of Ulster wasn't shaping up as they had thought. Ireland at that time wasn't a land of freedom but of turmoil and sectarian violence, so they turned west.

In the New World, the British colonies in Boston and beyond were very English, quite Anglican, and quite inhospitable to the Scots-Irish, most of whom were Celtic in culture and Presbyterian in faith. The frontiers all lay to the West and to the South, and, as it turns out, they chose both but came in much greater numbers to the South. The Appalachians lay beyond Virginia and in those mountains and beyond thousands of hardy Scots-Irish immigrants carved out lives for themselves and in so doing created the South as we know it today. They brought their music and songs, which in turn became bluegrass and country music. They brought their close-knit clan culture, they brought their strong religious faith, which in turn created the "Bible belt" as we know it today and they brought their famous sense of hospitality. Such was the legacy of the past and yet signposts of this past are still very obvious in the Southern culture today. Now, if we fast forward to the late twentieth century and beyond, how does this play out?

Today, visitors to the South don't arrive in tall ships or mule-drawn wagons over mountain paths but instead they arrive into the world's busiest airport in Atlanta, to a city of gleaming glass and steel; and in our case, when we arrived fifteen years ago we were incredibly impressed with the speed of the society. Used to a much slower pace of life in Ireland we took some time to settle in, but settle we did, and all around us, particularly outside the city, we noticed that subtle, underlying Celtic culture I described above.

One particular incident we remember well was a Fourth of July family party we were invited to in the country. An extended family that had been in the South for generations came together for a feast on the Fourth. We ate and laughed around tables in the yard, then after the wonderful meal, two uncles produced instruments and they began to sing and clap. We were amazed how Celtic the flavor of the entire event was. We felt so at home and were imagining that we could have been at *any* Sunday family gathering in rural Ireland! Then the idea for this book came to me. Why not create a book that celebrates this obvious cultural overlap that somehow seems hidden in plain sight?

And so, in this chapter we will begin that journey by setting out from Northern Ireland and sailing to America to do just that. We'll see how Irish griddle breads became corn bread. How scones became Southern biscuits. How hot tea became iced tea. How Irish whiskey was added to coffee to create the famous brew that everyone enjoys on March 17, and much, much more. So let's set sail and we'll discover the Irish coming to America!

October Glory Pumpkin and Lentil Soup
with cinnamon croutons and crème fraiche

The Story:

Pumpkins were one of those American icons that amazed us during our first few autumns in the United States. The pumpkin patches with their bright orange gourds were a delight to the eyes amongst the turning leaves and completely unusual to us. At Halloween in Ireland, we as children had to scoop the insides of turnips out to make lanterns, which was hard work indeed. We only wished we had these wonderful pumpkins instead!

This classic American autumnal vegetable soup encompasses New World flavors of pumpkin yet conjures up many memories with my Irish taste buds and reminds me of a combination of warm gingerbread and puréed root vegetables. The sweet and earthy flavors in this soup will warm your heart and soul as the cooler fall weather sets in.

Pumpkin & lentil soup ingredients (serves 6):
- 1 medium onion (finely chopped)
- 2 Tbsp. butter
- 1 tsp. fresh root ginger (peeled and grated)
- 7 oz. (1 cup) lentils (rinsed and soaked)
- 2 ½ pints (5 cups) vegetable stock
- 1 lb. peeled pumpkin or a 16-oz. can of pumpkin purée
- 4 oz. (½ cup) soft brown sugar
- 1 tsp. fine sea salt
- dash of freshly ground black pepper
- 1 tsp. cinnamon
- ¼ tsp. freshly grated
- ¼ cup heavy whipping cream

Cinnamon croutons ingredients:
- six ¼" slices of rustic baguette
- 3 Tbsp. butter (room temperature)
- 1 Tbsp. brown sugar
- ¼ tsp. cinnamon

Garnish ingredients:
- 3–4 Tbsp. crème fraiche (to garnish)
- pinch of kosher salt
- squeeze of lemon juice

How to make it:
1. Soak the lentils for a few hours beforehand to remove any foreign materials.
2. Melt the butter in a large saucepan on medium heat and sauté the onions until fragrant and translucent.
3. Add the fresh root ginger and sauté for a few more minutes with the onions.
4. Add the stock, lentils, pumpkin, brown sugar, salt, pepper, cinnamon, and nutmeg, stirring well.
5. Bring to a boil and then reduce the heat. Cover and simmer for 30 minutes, stirring occasionally until the lentils are soft.
6. Purée the soup with a food mill or liquidize in a blender.
7. Transfer the soup to a saucepan and slowly heat through. Stir in the cream and taste to adjust seasoning.
8. To make the cinnamon croutons, preheat the oven to 350°. Blend the butter, cinnamon, and brown sugar together then spread over the bread slices.
9. Bake for 5–7 minutes until crispy then chop into nuggets with a knife.
10. Prepare the garnish by blending a little kosher salt with lemon juice, mixing them into the crème fraiche.
11. Serve the soup in warmed bowls with a dollop of the crème fraiche mixture and a small handful of croutons.

fig and fennel skillet cornbread
with Irish cheddar cheese

the story:

The Creek Indians in Tennessee and Georgia were using corn in all sorts of ways for generations before European settlers arrived, and given its versatility it's no wonder the new arrivals picked up on this staple and blended it with their homeland techniques. The simple list of ingredients found in this famous Southern quick bread resembles Irish soda or Wheaten, and I cannot help but imagine how the Scots-Irish settlers improvised and adapted to the newfound colorful cornmeal. I love the crunchy outside contrasted with the soft cake-like consistency of this bread, while the fennel seeds provide an interesting liquorish flavor that blends perfectly with the sweet figs and salty cheese!

Ingredients (serves 4–6):

- 2 Tbsp. melted butter (or bacon fat)
- 6 oz. (1 ½ cup) all-purpose flour (sifted)
- 4 oz. (1 cup) stone ground cornmeal
- 2 Tbsp. sugar
- 2 tsp. baking powder (sifted)
- ½ tsp. salt
- 4 oz. (1 cup) aged Irish cheddar cheese (grated)
- 8 fl. oz. (1 cup) buttermilk
- 4 Tbsp. vegetable oil (you can substitute melted butter)
- 1 egg (beaten)
- 5 figs (cut into eighths)
- 1 Tbsp. fennel seeds

How to make it:

1. Preheat the oven to 400°.
2. Grease a small 8" cast iron skillet or 8" baking pan with butter.
3. Place the cast iron skillet into the oven to preheat.
4. Combine the flour, cornmeal, sugar, salt, and baking powder in mixing bowl. Stir in the cheese and fennel seeds.
5. In another bowl, whisk together the buttermilk, egg, and vegetable oil. Combine the wet and dry ingredients together and stir with a large metal spoon to mix.
6. Remove the preheated skillet from the oven and pour in the batter.
7. Press figs into batter and arrange in a circular fashion.
8. Bake the cornbread for 25 minutes.
9. Remove from the oven and set skillet on a rack to cool for 10 minutes before slicing and serving.

Southern Mountain Biscuits with Chives and Cheddar

The Story:

In Ireland, what we call "savory scones" a true Southerner eats for dinner and calls them "biscuits." At first I could not get used to the idea, but these melt-in-your-mouth biscuits have changed my thinking. It seems that the same basic recipe and idea came across the Atlantic and morphed into these Southern delights. Cooks in the South pride themselves on the fluffiness and the whiteness of their biscuits, and these flavorful delights work well with a combination of other flavors. Famous with chicken and gravy, they are also commonly served at breakfast. This again is an old recipe from a Southern friend from the mountains of North Georgia.

Southern biscuits ingredients (makes 12 biscuits):

- 8 oz. (2 cups) self-rising flour (sifted)
- 1/8 tsp. baking soda
- 3 oz. shortening (cold and cut into pieces)
- 2 oz. (½ cup) aged Irish cheddar cheese (finely grated)
- 1 Tbsp. chives (finely chopped)
- ½ pint (1 cup) buttermilk
- 2 Tbsp. butter (melted to brush)
- garlic salt (to sprinkle)

How to make it:

1. Preheat your oven to 450°.
2. Sift the flour and soda into a bowl then cut in shortening until the mixture resembles coarse crumbs.
3. Stir in the cheese and chives.
4. Blend in the buttermilk and stir until the dough leaves the sides of the bowl.
5. Place the dough on a lightly floured surface and knead gently 2 or 3 times.
6. Roll the dough out to ½" thick with a lightly floured rolling pin then, using a biscuit cutter, cut into 12 large biscuits.
7. Place the biscuits, almost touching, on large baking tray for soft sides. If you prefer crispy sides, place 1" apart on the baking tray.
8. Brush the tops of the biscuits with melted butter.
9. Bake for 10–12 minutes until golden brown.
10. Brush with more melted butter then sprinkle with a little garlic salt. Best served warm.

Southern Fried Green Tomato Stack
with Irish blue cheese, topped with a balsamic syrup and peach & onion jam

The Story:

It seems like every Southern cook knows how to fry up these beauties in the summer months in Georgia. Being Irish, I was already familiar with fried tomatoes but only the ripe red variety fried in a pan with an Ulster Fry; the green variety, so famous in the South, at first seemed a little strange. They're certainly much more tart in flavor, but I soon adapted this New World variation and claimed it as an Ulster Kitchen favorite.

In this recipe I add some tangy blue cheese into the stack to make these crunchy tomatoes really sing, as well adding a little sweet peach and onion jam to the mix to balance it out and yet enhance the flavors. I think you'll enjoy this one!

Fried green tomatoes ingredients (serves 4 as an appetizer):

- 4 large green tomatoes
- coarse sea salt and pepper
- 3 oz. (¾ cups) stone ground cornmeal
- 3 oz. (¾ cups) all-purpose flour
- 2 eggs (beaten)
- 4 fl. oz. (½ cup) buttermilk
- vegetable oil (to fry)
- 2 Tbsp. basil (chopped)
- 4 oz. (1 cup) Irish blue cheese

Balsamic syrup

- 8 fl. oz. (1 cup) dark balsamic vinegar

Peach and onion jam ingredients:

- 1 Tbsp. olive oil
- 1 medium onion (1 cup finely chopped)
- 2 lbs. peaches (2 ¼ cups peeled and diced)
- 3 Tbsp. white wine vinegar
- 3 Tbsp. brown sugar
- ½ tsp. ground ginger
- ½ tsp. smoked paprika
- ½ tsp. ground cumin
- ½ tsp. kosher salt
- ¼ tsp. ground black pepper

How to make it:

1. To make the peach and onion jam, heat some oil over a medium-high heat and gently fry the onions for 3 minutes or until soft.
2. Stir in the peaches, brown sugar, vinegar, and spices then bring to a simmer.
3. Cover and cook for 8–10 minutes then remove from the heat and allow to cool.
4. To make the balsamic syrup, place the vinegar in a small saucepan and gently boil until it is reduced by 75%.
5. Remove from heat and set aside.
6. 6. Slice the green tomatoes into generous ¼" pieces and season with coarse sea salt and ground black pepper.
7. Beat the eggs and buttermilk together with a fork.
8. Mix the flours together in a small bowl then dip each slice of tomato into the wet mixture, shaking off the excess, and coat them in the dry flour mixture.
9. Heat some oil in a heavy cast iron skillet to medium-high temperature.
10. Avoiding crowding, place a few slices of tomato at a time into the skillet, frying them for about 3 minutes on each side.
11. When done, place each slice on a warmed plate.
12. Assemble by placing a little peach and onion jam in center of your plate then stacking the tomatoes with a slice of blue cheese between each tomato layer, ending with a little cheese on top and a teaspoon more of the peach and onion jam.
13. Sprinkle on top a little freshly chopped basil.
14. Best served immediately.

peachy mint iced Irish Tea
with Plantation mint and Georgia peaches

the story:

In the South, folks seem to drink as much tea as the Irish, but only as a refreshing iced beverage instead of the customary hot *cuppa* served on cold Irish days. Of course, this cultural shift is climate-driven more than anything else and after living in the Deep South for many years, we can see why. The strength and flavor of Irish tea when iced and blended with fruit juices and Southern plantation mint can be incredibly refreshing in the "Hotlanta" heat. I serve this iced tea at parties throughout the summer and have to say that it is as visually appealing as it is delicious in taste.

For the simple sugar syrup:
- 1 pint (2 cups) sugar
- 2 pints (4 cups) water

Iced tea ingredients (makes 7 cups or 3 ½ pints):
- 2 pints (4 cups) natural spring water
- generous handful of mint sprigs (8 sprigs, plus more to garnish the glasses)
- 4 bags of Irish breakfast tea (decaf or regular)
- 1 pint (2 cups) peach nectar
- ½ pint (1 cup) simple syrup (as above)
- fresh peach slices (to garnish)

How to make it:
1. Make the simple sugar syrup by bringing the sugar and water to a boil in a medium-sized saucepan.
2. Boil for a few minutes until the sugar has completely dissolved.
3. Cool the resulting syrup and set aside. (The simple syrup can be stored in refrigerator for several weeks).
4. Bring 4 cups of water to a boil.
5. Add the mint sprigs and boil for 1 more minute.
6. Remove from the heat and pour the boiling mint water over the tea bags. Cover and infuse for 3–4 minutes. (Do not over-steep, as all black tea takes on a bitter taste if not infused correctly.)
7. Strain and discard the mint and the tea bags.
8. Set aside to cool slightly.
9. In a large pitcher, stir in the peach nectar, simple syrup, and tea.
10. Cover and chill for 4–6 hours or overnight in the refrigerator.
11. Serve over crushed ice.
12. To garnish, place a slit in a peach slice and slide the slice onto the edge of each glass. Add a sprig of fresh mint.

St. Patrick's Colcannon & Corned Beef

potatoes, American corned beef, curly kale, and a parsley cheese sauce

The Story:

Most Americans are shocked when I tell them that my first meal exposure to the infamous St. Patrick's meal of corned beef and cabbage was when I moved to the USA. What *we* refer to as *corned beef* in Ireland comes in a tin and is a rather unsavory entrée choice, but in America corned beef is a brined, cured beef that is delicious and has its origins with the Irish immigrants in the Americas who brined beef as they did pork back in old Ireland.

Colcannon potatoes ingredients:

- 2 ½ lbs. potatoes (floury variety)
- 4 Tbsp. (¼ cup) milk
- 7 oz. curly kale (hard stalks removed)
- 8 spring onions (finely chopped)
- 1 ½ tsp. sea salt
- ¼ tsp. black pepper
- 4 oz. (1/2 cup) unsalted Irish butter
- 4 fl. oz. (½ cup) heavy whipping cream
- 4 fl. oz. (¼ cup) reserved cooking liquid from kale

Corned beef ingredients:

- 1 ½ lb. flat cut brined corned beef
- a little olive oil

Parsley cheese sauce ingredients:

- 2 oz. butter
- 2 oz. flour
- ½ pint (1 cup) whole milk
- ¼ pint (½ cup) chicken stock
- 1 oz. (1/4 cup) Dubliner Irish cheese (grated)
- 1 tsp. Dijon mustard
- handful of curly parsley (leafy part only and finely chopped)
- curly parsley sprigs (for garnish)

How to make it:

1. To cook the brisket, preheat oven to 300°, then wrap up the brisket like a parcel inside a sheet of foil, fat side up.
2. Drizzle a little olive oil over and roast for 1 hour per pound, leaving 15 minutes for the meat to rest before carving.
3. To make the Colcannon, place the potatoes in a large pan of cold, salted water with milk, adding just enough water to cover potatoes.
4. Bring to a boil and then reduce the heat and simmer for about 20 minutes until the potatoes are soft when pierced with a fork.
5. Drain the potatoes with a metal strainer then set the potatoes back on the warm stovetop to allow them to dry out a little.
6. In a large saucepan, bring some water to a roaring boil and blanch the kale for 1 minute.
7. Drain the kale, retaining the cooking liquid, and place the kale in a blender, pulsing for a few seconds.
8. Melt the butter with the cream and the retained cooking liquid from the kale. Infuse the spring onions, cooking for 30 seconds to soften.
9. Mash potatoes and slowly add the resulting liquid. Fold in the kale, salt, and pepper.
10. Prepare the parsley sauce by melting the butter in a small saucepan. Add the flour and allow to cook gently for 1 minute, stirring constantly. Whisk in the milk and chicken stock and bring sauce to a simmer and cook for 3–4 minutes. Stir in the cheese and mustard and cook for 1 more minute. Season with salt and pepper and stir in chopped parsley.
11. To serve, spoon the potatoes onto a warmed plate. Place slices of corned beef on top. Drizzle meat and dish with about 2 Tbsp. of parsley sauce.
12. Garnish with a small sprig of curly parsley and serve immediately.

Coke-soaked Braised venison
with creamy potato and parsnip mash

the story:

We have a generous Southern friend who enjoys sport shooting and supplies us with venison during the hunting season here in Georgia. He was also generous enough with us to share his unique marinade for venison using Atlanta-born Coca-Cola to tenderize the meat. To an Irish immigrant such as I, this was such an unusual meal concept but one which tasted surprisingly delicious, and I just *had* to include it in this "Coming to America" chapter. I am sure those early Scots-Irish immigrants also had their fair share of deer hunting as they settled the Appalachians! Enjoy!

Coke marinade ingredients (serves 4):

- 2 fl. oz (1/4 cup) coke
- 2 Tbsp. vegetable oil
- 1 Tbsp. soy sauce
- 1 Tbsp. Worchester sauce
- 1 garlic clove (crushed)
- ¼ tsp. freshly milled black pepper
- ¼ tsp. kosher salt

Venison stew ingredients:

- 3 slices of thick cut bacon
- 1 Tbsp. olive oil
- 2 lbs. venison back strap (cut into 2" strips)
- 4 Tbsp. all purpose flour
- ½ tsp. kosher salt
- ¼ tsp. pepper
- 3 medium onions (peeled and thickly sliced)
- 4 carrots (peeled and cut into 1" strips)
- 12 fl. oz. (1 ½ cups) red wine
- 1 pint (2 cups) beef stock
- 2 Tbsp. red currant jelly
- 2 Tbsp. tomato purée
- sprig of thyme (1 tsp. chopped)
- 2 bay leaves

Parsnip and potato mash ingredients:

- 5 medium-sized potatoes (cut into 1" pieces)
- 3 medium-sized parsnips (scraped and cut into 1" pieces)
- 2 oz. (1/4 cup) butter
- 6 Tbsp. heavy whipping cream
- ½ tsp. salt
- ¼ tsp. white pepper
- pinch of grated fresh nutmeg

How to make Coke-soaked Braised Venison:

1. Combine the ingredients for marinade together and soak the venison in this marinade overnight in a zip-lock bag.
2. In a large skillet, cook the bacon until crisp then remove the bacon from pan.
3. Remove the meat from the marinate and drain.
4. Toss the marinated venison meat in flour seasoned with salt and pepper.
5. Preheat oven to 350° F.
6. Drain off a little bacon grease, reserving 2 Tbsp. for sautéing.
7. Heat the remaining fat to medium-hot and add the meat to the skillet in small batches, searing for 2–3 minutes on each side.
8. Transfer to a Dutch-style oven or deep casserole dish with a lid.
9. Add a little oil to the skillet and sauté the onions until soft before adding carrots and cook for 2 more minutes.
10. Transfer the vegetables to the dish with the seared meat.
11. Deglaze the skillet with the red wine. Add the stock, thyme, bay leaves, tomato purée, and red currant jelly, stirring to combine.
12. Pour the resulting liquid over the meat and vegetables, place in the oven, and bake for 1 hour.
13. Add bacon and cook for 15 more minutes, then remove the bay leaves and discard.
14. To serve, place a large spoonful of parsnip and potato mash in center of the plate, making a well. Spoon the venison stew into the potato parsnip nest and garnish.

How to make Parsnip and potato mash:

1. Place the potatoes and parsnips into a medium saucepan with enough cold water to cover the vegetables.
2. Bring to a boil and cook for 15 minutes until soft.
3. Drain vegetables then run through a potato ricer before mashing with butter, cream, salt, pepper, and nutmeg.

Ulster American Apple and Blackberry Tart

The story:

What could be more classically American and also classically Ulster than the apple pie? Known as *apple tarts* in Northern Ireland these pies are a great tradition in the part of Ireland I am from, County Armagh, also known as the *Apple County*. In the autumn I spend an entire Saturday baking these for my freezer so I can enjoy them all winter. If you are like me and plan to make several to freeze, do not slit the top of the crust or bake; wait until you are ready, *then* prepare.

Back in Northern Ireland, my grandmother used to wrap money in silver foil and hide them in her tarts for us to find when we came to her house around Halloween time. Sometimes she used blackberries grown wild in the Irish hedgerow, and the results were just wonderful.

(Basic crust recipe)

- 8 oz. (2 cups) all-purpose flour
- pinch salt
- 6 oz. (¾ cups) shortening
- 7 Tbsp. iced water
- beaten egg and milk (to glaze)
- 1 tsp granulated sugar (to dust)

(Apple pie filling ingredients)

- 4 large tart apples (5 cups pealed, cored, and thinly sliced)
- 6 oz. (1 cup) blackberries
- 1 Tbsp. lemon juice
- 5 ¼ oz (¾ cup) fine granulated sugar
- 3 Tbsp. all-purpose flour
- ½ tsp. cinnamon
- 1/8 tsp. nutmeg
- good pinch ground cloves
- dash of salt
- 2 Tbsp. unsalted butter (cut in to small pieces)

How to make it:

1. Using a pastry cutter or food processor combine the flour, salt and the shortening by pulsing together for about 12-15 seconds or until the mixture comes together. Add the ice water until the mixture *comes away* from the sides of the bowl.

2. Cut the dough in half with a knife and work each piece with palm of your hands to make two circular balls. Gently press down using the palms of hands to form two circular discs. Refrigerate for 30 minutes to allow the dough to rest.

3. Next, prepare the filling by adding lemon juice to the prepared apples in a suitable bowl. Stir in the sugar, flour, cinnamon, nutmeg, cloves, salt, and blackberries.

4. When ready, roll out the first pastry ball on a lightly floured surface using a floured rolling pin to form a 12" circle. Gently ease the pastry into a 9" pie plate, folding any excess pastry under and trim.

5. Fill the pastry with the prepared apple and blackberry mixture and then *dot* the surface with butter.

6. Roll the remaining pastry ball to form another 12" circle and place it on top of the fruit, folding any excess pastry under and then trim with a sharp knife. For a fluted edge place your thumb against the inside of the pastry and press the dough around the thumb as if to pinch, using the other thumb and index finger or a fork to seal the edges. Cut a generous slit in the center to release air during baking.

7. Brush with a little beaten egg and milk and sprinkle with sugar.

8. Bake at 350° F on a foil-lined baking sheet (in case of juice spilling) for 50 minutes.

9. Best served warm with fresh whipped cream or vanilla ice cream.

A fine Irish-American coffee
Black coffee with whiskey & cream

The story:

Irish coffee is undoubtedly a beverage famous the world over and ever associated with Saint Patrick's Day celebrations. The combination of strong black coffee, brown sugar, Irish whiskey and cream is a genius combination. They can be a little tricky to make properly though, so I'm going to guide you through it!

As for the history of this most famous Irish brew, it may surprise you to know that Irish coffee is a relatively new tradition in Irish terms, created in 1943 by barman Joe Sheridan. The drink was first served to transatlantic passengers arriving on boats from the USA to Foynes in County Limerick, and it did not take long for the recipe to spread all over the island. The drink became even more famous in 1952 when a journalist from San Francisco visited Ireland and brought the recipe back home, passing it on to Jack Koeppler, owner of the Buena Vista. The drink was a huge hit, and the rest is history!

In Ireland, Irish coffee is traditionally served in a glass so you can see the dark coffee and whiskey base with the cream floating on top. The cream is lightly whipped and not beaten too thick so it will float on the top and not sink to the bottom of the glass.

An Irish coffee is a way we say *welcome* and offer hospitality in our home. It's definitely a celebratory drink and the perfect ending to a great meal.

Irish coffee ingredients (for 1 cup coffee):

- 4 fl. oz. (½ cup) strong, hot coffee
- 1–2 Tbsp. brown sugar (to taste)
- 2 fl. oz. (¼ cup) Irish whiskey
- 2 Tbsp. cream (lightly whipped)
- freshly ground nutmeg

How to make it:

1. Beat the heavy whipping cream with an electric beater until stiff. Set the cream aside in refrigerator until ready to serve coffee.
2. Heat a stemmed glass or coffee cup.
3. Place brown sugar in the bottom of the glass before adding the freshly brewed coffee. Stir together until dissolved.
4. Pour the Irish whiskey into the coffee and sugar.
5. Spoon the prepared freshly whipped cream *lightly* on top of the coffee in the glass.
6. Sprinkle a little freshly ground nutmeg on top. *Do not stir.*
7. Drink right way and say "Sliante!" (that's Irish for Cheers!).

Antebellum home, Roswell Georgia

My grandmother's tea set named 'Atlanta'

the Southern Tea

Tea in the South is an honored tradition
with beautiful things, cherished friends,
wonderful food and good conversation

Tea time delights, gingerbread scones & clotted cream

Having tea with my sister Claire, and my niece Susie

The Southern Tea: An Ancient Art

One of the many peculiarities and joys of living in the South is found in the discovery that many of the old traditions of a more refined, bygone age have survived the modern era. One such example is found in the Southern tea culture and the exquisite tearooms that go along with it.

Tea drinking came from those early English settlers that colonized America as Puritans and Quakers back in the day. It was William Penn who introduced tea drinking to the Quaker colony he founded in Delaware in 1682, and tea drinking has formed part of the fabric of this great country ever since. Tea drinking *did* go into somewhat of a decline, however, in the latter part of the twentieth century as the automobile culture and the faster-paced life that went along with it took hold, and the more relaxed ethos of tea drinking became somewhat of a relic. However, amongst all the hustle and bustle that defined America in the mid-twentieth century, one region retained this ancient tradition: namely, the South.

As I mentioned in earlier chapters, the overarching influence of the inherited Celtic culture in the South did a lot to shape the prevailing culture in the South today, and perhaps the survival of the ancient tradition of tea drinking and of the Southern tearooms has a lot to do with that. We know that traditional Southern hospitality and the art form of conversation survived in the South despite the onslaught of the twentieth century, so it stands to reason to assume that the wonders of the Southern tea also owe a lot to that Celtic overtone.

When we settled in Georgia, we were pleasantly surprised by the existence of tearooms and of all the finery that went with them. After living in the northeast for two years, we assumed that the drive-through coffee and doughnut culture was the prevailing American culture everywhere. We did not expect tearooms with delicate sandwiches or refined ladies with large hats and high heels, but here they were. I distinctly remember one early Southern experience when a lady and her mother invited me to an afternoon tea in her home in Roswell, Georgia. I must confess, I *was* expecting doughnuts and coffee and would have been happy with that but instead was treated to the most exquisite tea experience, just as beautiful as any in Ireland. Beautiful raised platters hosted delicate savory sandwiches and delightful sweet treats of many kinds. The ladies were dressed beautifully in dresses and heels and the table was prepared with thought and care; I was thrilled at the fine china, folded lace napkins, flowers, and—to my amazement—the most delicious hot tea served in decorated teacups.

As you can now imagine, I was blessed and honored almost to tears and have never forgotten that first exposure to the ancient tradition of afternoon tea in the South. It reminded me of home, of the hospitality of Northern Ireland that I had assumed I had left behind, and I was overcome with joy to discover that this culture was alive and well. Little did my friends know it, but they were reviving something important that American society seemed to need. In an age of fast food, abrupt service, and interrupting cell phones, the serenity of having tea is an oasis. It is no wonder that today hundreds of tearooms are springing up across the United States as people long for something different, something refined, and something to experience for more than just a few minutes.

In this chapter I will continue to celebrate this wonderful tradition that is alive and well in the South and provide you with some of my most requested teatime favorites. We'll nibble our way through roast beef and cucumber sandwiches, caramel squares, butterfly cupcakes, and gingerbread scones and round it all off with some Georgia peach fools. So let me invite you to dress up, don those heels, find your most fabulous hat, wear those pearls, and we shall have *tea*, y'all!

queen of the south chicken salads
a celebration on both sides of the Atlantic

the story:

Coronation Chicken Salad was created to mark the ascension of Princess Elizabeth to the throne in 1953, while *Southern Chicken Salad* is its Southern cousin. Both equally delicious, these two differing chicken fillings are enjoyed in plenty of coffee houses and tearooms in each region, and in the spirit of fusion that this book brings, I'm presenting to you the best of both worlds. I have added toasted pecans to the Coronation recipe for a touch of the American South.

Try serving these salads on a bed of mixed organic greens, or as a filling inside phyllo pastry, or in toasted croissants rolls. Either way, they are a versatile recipe to add to your teatime repertoire.

Southern style ingredients (with almonds and tarragon; serves 4):

- 4 cooked chicken breasts (cut into bite-sized pieces)
- 1 oz. silvered almonds (toasted)
- 1 Tbsp. fresh tarragon (chopped)
- small bunch (½ cup) red seedless grapes (cut in half)

Dressing ingredients:

- 4 fl. oz. (½ cup) mayonnaise
- juice of ½ lemon
- 2 Tbsp. honey
- salt and pepper to taste

How to make it:

1. Whisk together all the dressing ingredients.
2. Combine the dressing with the chicken, almonds, and tarragon.
3. Fold in grapes and refrigerate until ready to eat.

Coronation style ingredients (with apricots and pecans; serves 4):

- 4 cooked chicken breasts (cut into bite-sized pieces)
- 2 green onions (finely chopped)
- 1 stalk celery (finely chopped)
- 1 oz. (¼ cup) pecans (chopped and toasted)

Dressing ingredients:

- 2 oz. (1/3 cup) dried apricots (soaked in water overnight)
- 4 fl. oz. (½ cup) mayonnaise
- juice of ½ lemon
- 2 Tbsp. mango chutney
- 2 tsp. Indian curry paste or powder
- salt and pepper (to taste)

How to make it:

- Drain any excess liquid from the soaked apricots and purée in a blender.
- Add the remaining dressing ingredients to apricots and then fold in the chicken, green onions, pecans, and celery.
- Refrigerate until ready.

Southern wonder cucumber sandwiches
with dry roasted Southern peanuts and cream cheese

The story:

No classic tea menu is ever complete without the cucumber sandwich! Here we have given our traditional teatime staple a new Southern twist by adding some dry roasted Georgia peanuts, which not only add a little protein but a delicious salty, crunchy texture. Combine this with a little cream cheese, and you have a new spin on an old recipe. Serve on a silver platter and the bragging rights will be yours!

Southern wonder cucumber sandwich ingredients (makes 8 sandwiches):

(For the cucumber sandwich)
- ¼ of a large cucumber (English seedless variety)
- 1 Tbsp. white wine vinegar
- ½ tsp. salt
- 1 Tbsp. unsalted butter (softened)
- 4 slices of white bread (thinly cut)

(For the cream cheese filling)
- 4 oz. (½ cup) cream cheese (room temperature)
- 1 oz. (¼ cup) dry roasted peanuts (finely chopped)
- 2 Tbsp. local honey

How to make them:

1. To prepare the cucumber, remove the skin and then slice as finely as possible in long strips using a sharp knife or a potato peeler.
2. Sprinkle the thin slices with the vinegar and salt, then marinate for 30 minutes.
3. While the cucumber is marinating, prepare the cream cheese filling by blending the cream cheese and honey by hand or in a food processor, then fold in the chopped, dry roasted peanuts.
4. Drain any excess cucumber juice using a sieve and pat gently dry with some paper towels.
5. Butter the slices of bread then spread with the cream cheese mixture.
6. Layer the slices of the cucumber on top of the cream cheese then press the second layer of bread on top, pressing down gently using the palm of your hand.
7. Slice off the crusts cleanly with an electric knife or bread knife and cut each sandwich into 4 small, thin rectangles or squares.
8. Cover with a lightly dampened cloth and keep stored in the refrigerator until ready to serve.

celtic GOLD checkered sandwiches
with carrots, cheese, and apple

the story:

Another great vegetarian option for your afternoon tea party, these delightful sandwiches are a treat to the eyes as well as the palate, with the colors of the ingredients giving a fun nod to all things green, gold, and Celtic. Interestingly light and refreshing, the sandwiches can be served standing upright so guests can see the golden filling. I would recommend that you make these sandwiches the day of the event, but they can be prepared the night before if refrigerated and covered with a slightly damp tea towel.

Celtic gold sandwich ingredients (makes 8 tea sandwiches):

(For the sandwich)
- 2 slices of soft white bread
- 2 slices of brown wheat bread
- 1 Tbsp. unsalted butter (softened)

(For the filling)
- 2 small carrots (¾ cup finely grated)
- 1 small apple (¼ cup grated)
- 1 tsp. lemon juice
- 2 oz. (½ cup) sharp white Irish cheddar cheese (finely grated)
- 1 Tbsp. parsley (finely chopped)
- 2 Tbsp. mayo
- pinch of salt and pepper

How to make them:
1. To make the filling, scrape the carrots and grate them finely in a food processor or by hand using a box grater. Then peel the apple and grate, adding a little lemon juice to avoid discoloration. Finally, grate the cheese.
2. Combine the grated carrot, apple, and cheese together, then stir in the parsley and mayo. Season to taste and refrigerate.
3. Spread some butter thinly to the edges of the bread to protect the sandwich from becoming soggy.
4. To assemble, use a knife to spread the filling over the slices of white buttered bread then press the remaining slices of wheat bread gently on top, using the palms of your hands to seal.
5. Use a sharp knife to remove the crusts and then cut the bread into four even triangles.

Roast Beef Sandwiches with Caramelized Onion

with roasted red peppers and a spicy mustard sauce

The story:

Although roast beef sandwiches may be considered very *Old World*, the addition of caramelized Vidalia onions, roasted red peppers, and spicy mustard sauce give these teatime favorites a distinctly Southern edge. As I host tea party events with the Ulster Kitchen, I repeatedly find that these wonderful sandwiches are in great demand. The combination of flavors, textures, and colors works so well together and provides an interesting, warm alternative to the cooler flavored cucumber and salad offerings typical at a party.

Sandwich ingredients (makes 8 sandwiches):

- 4 slices of roast beef (thinly sliced or shaved at the deli)
- 1 Tbsp. olive oil
- ½ medium Vidalia onion
- 2 slices of multigrain brown bread (crusts removed)
- 1 Tbsp. unsalted butter (softened)

Sauce ingredients:

- 2 Tbsp. mayonnaise
- 1 tsp. sour cream
- 1 tsp. wholegrain spicy mustard
- ½ tsp. horseradish sauce

Garnish ingredients:

- eight ½" strips roasted red pepper (optional for garnish)
- small sprig of thyme (8 tiny pieces)
- kosher salt and freshly ground black pepper

How to make them:

1. Thinly slice the onion and sauté with a little olive oil in a pan over medium heat until they are caramelized. Set aside.
2. To make the sauce, combine the mayonnaise, Dijon mustard, horseradish sauce, and sour cream together in a small bowl.
3. Lightly butter each slice of bread to the edges to protect the bread from becoming soggy, and then remove the crusts from the outside.
4. Cut each slice of bread into four triangles.
5. To assemble the sandwiches, spread 1 tsp. of sauce onto the buttered bread then bunch a ½ slice of roast beef on top of each slice of bread. Sprinkle on a pinch of salt and some freshly ground black pepper then top with a little caramelized onion. Add a thin strip of roasted red pepper for color and a tiny sprig of thyme for garnish.

Gingerbread Scones with Clotted Lemon Cream

The Story:

Ginger and cream are a scrumptious combination any time of the year, but I especially love to serve them for tea around the Christmas holiday season. The aromas of the spices as they bake in the oven are both heartwarming and festive! Gingerbread is an Old World recipe that has somehow become synonymous with America, so I thought it was very fitting to include this wonderful recipe in this chapter. These delightful scones are always a hit with my patrons at Ulster Kitchen tea events, and I usually serve them in halves topped with a generous blob of home-style clotted lemon cream!

Gingerbread scone ingredients (makes ½ dozen):

- 1 lb. (4 cups) self-rising flour
- 1 tsp. baking powder
- 2 oz. (¼ cup) dark brown sugar
- ¼ tsp. salt
- 1 tsp. ground powdered ginger
- ½ tsp. nutmeg
- ¾ tsp. cinnamon
- 6 oz. (¾ cup) butter (cold and cut into small pieces)
- 1 egg (beaten)
- 4 fl. oz. (½ cup) buttermilk
- 2 fl. oz. (¼ cup) molasses
- egg wash (1 egg beaten with a little water or milk)

Clotted lemon cream ingredients (makes just over a cup):

- 3 oz. cream cheese (softened to room temperature)
- 1 Tbsp. fine granulated sugar
- zest of 1 lemon
- pinch of kosher salt
- 8 fl. oz. (1 cup) heavy whipping cream

How to make the cream:

1. In an electric mixer, combine the cream cheese, lemon zest, sugar, and salt.
2. On low speed, combine the heavy whipping cream into the mixture, being careful not to over-beat, until cream mixture becomes stiff.
3. Refrigerate until ready to serve.

How to make Gingerbread:

1. Preheat your oven to 425° F.
2. Sift the flour with the baking powder then combine the remaining dry ingredients together in a food processor or a large mixing bowl.
3. Cut the cold butter into the mixed dry ingredients then rub the mixture together with your fingertips or add them slowly to a food processor to form a breadcrumb-like texture.
4. Beat the buttermilk, egg, and molasses together in a small bowl and combine with the dry ingredients, mixing well.
5. Turn the resulting dough out onto a lightly floured surface.
6. Knead the dough a few times and then roll it out with a lightly floured rolling pin until it's about ¾" thick.
7. Cut the scones out of the flattened dough using a 1" biscuit cutter.
8. Brush dough scones with egg wash and place onto a lightly greased baking sheet.
9. Bake 12–15 minutes until well risen and golden brown on top, turning the baking tray halfway through baking time to ensure even baking.
10. Best served warm. Serve sliced in half and slathered with clotted cream.

Georgia Peach Fool Shots

the story:

A fruit *fool* is a creamy dessert that is popular in Ireland, made with poached fruit. My grandmother used to make them in the summer with puréed apples, gooseberries, and rhubarb. The name, which sounds quite odd, probably comes from the French word *fouler*, which means *to crush* or *to squash*. I love to make them with peaches during Georgia's summer season but have found that canned peaches work equally well, so you can enjoy making these little shots any time of the year.

Georgia peach fool ingredients (makes 12 shots):

(For the peach purée)
- 6 peaches
- 3 Tbsp. peach flavor liqueur
- 3 Tbsp. water
- 4 oz. (¼ cup) sugar

(For the cream)
- 8 fl. oz. (1 cup) heavy whipping cream
- 4 fl. oz. (½ cup) mascarpone cream
- 8 oz. (½ cup) fine granulated sugar

(For the garnish)
- mint sprigs

How to make them

1. If using fresh peaches, remove the skins with a sharp knife and remove the stones, then combine the peaches, sugar, and water in a small saucepan.
2. Cook on a medium heat to gently poach for 8–10 minutes or until the peaches are tender.
3. Cool and then chill in a refrigerator.
4. When the peaches are cool, add the peach liqueur to the mixture and purée in a food processor. (If using canned peaches, drain the syrup from the can using a sieve *then* purée with the peach flavor liqueur.)
5. Beat the cream and sugar until it forms *soft peaks* in an electric mixer.
6. Soften the mascarpone cheese by beating gently by hand then fold it into the fresh cream, being careful not to over-beat the mixture. Try to ensure a smooth, creamy texture.
7. Gently combine about one third of the purée, leaving swirls of peach purée.
8. Spoon the cream mixture into a piping bag with a large nozzle.
9. Spoon 1 ½ tsp. of reserved purée into the bottom of each glass and then pipe some cream into the individual glasses. Place a second layer of purée on top, followed by cream, then finish with a little more purée.
10. Pipe a final decorative swirl of cream on top.
11. Refrigerate for at least 2 hours.
12. Garnish with a tiny sprig of mint.

Sweet and Salty Caramel Squares

The Story:

Caramel shortbread squares are a very common "tray bake" in Northern Ireland, found in the display cases of every home bakery and coffee shop throughout the province. In fact, when we return, they are one of the foods we love to indulge in, as we associate them so closely with "home". However, for this creation I have taken the traditional Ulster recipe and added some American salty pretzels to the mix, and to me this is a complete revelation! They are a super-rich, indulgent treat, but how can anyone possibly resist shortbread, salty caramel, and chocolate, I ask you?

Caramel Squares ingredients (makes 2½ dozen squares):

(Shortbread base ingredients)
- 2 cups (8 oz.) self-rising flour
- 3 oz. (3 Tbsp.) fine granulated sugar
- 6 oz. (¾ cup) butter (softened)
- 1–2 Tbsp. milk

(Carmel Layer)
- 4 oz. (½ cup) butter
- 14 fl. oz. can of sweetened condensed milk
- 4 Tbsp. (¼ cup) sugar
- 2 Tbsp. golden cane syrup
- handful of pretzels (1 oz. roughly chopped)

(Chocolate Topping ingredients)
- 3 oz. (6 Tbsp.) butter
- 7 oz. milk chocolate (1 cup) chocolate chips

How to make them:

1. Preheat your oven to 325° F. Then grease a 13x9" baking pan.
2. Sift the flour then cream the butter and sugar together in an electric mixer or by hand.
3. Add the flour and *just enough* milk to form the dough, then allow to rest for 30 minutes in the refrigerator.
4. Remove the dough from the refrigerator and cut into four pieces.
5. Roll out each piece thinly with a floured rolling pin in a rectangular shape, then join the pieces of dough together in the baking pan, pressing firmly and evenly with your fingers and palm of hand to fill the pan. Prick the shortbread all over with a fork to ensure even baking.
6. Bake for 25–30 minutes until the pastry is a light golden brown color.
7. To make the caramel, combine all the ingredients together in a heavy-based saucepan. Place over a medium to low heat and stir continuously until boiling.
8. Boil for 6–7 minutes until the caramel thickens enough to leave the side of pan, stirring all the time.
9. Once the caramel is ready, fold in the chopped pretzels.
10. Spread the caramel over the cooled shortbread with a small spatula or knife.
11. When the caramel layer has set, melt the chocolate and butter in a double boiler over low heat. Remove from heat and stir until smooth. Cool slightly before spreading over the caramel layer with a knife.
12. When chocolate is firm and set, cut into fingers or squares.

Victoria Sandwich Butterfly Cupcakes
served with vanilla cream

The Story:

My grandmother always served a Victoria sandwich cake for afternoon tea at her guesthouse in County Down, Northern Ireland, with fresh cream and jam or fruit purée in the cake filling. Named after the famous queen, it remains an old-fashioned jewel using the simple ingredients of butter, flour, and eggs with a hint of lemon. I have given this refreshingly light, very traditional Old World cake recipe a new American spin by morphing it into these delicious cupcakes, served with strawberries, vanilla cream, and a fun butterfly decoration that will look great on your tea party table.

Ingredients (makes 24 cupcakes):

(For the sponge)

- 8 oz. (1 cup) soft margarine (room temperature)
- 8 oz. (1 cup) fine granulated sugar
- 4 eggs (beaten at room temperature)
- 8 oz. (2 cups) self-rising flour (sifted)
- 1 tsp. baking powder (sifted with flour)
- 1 tsp. grated lemon rind
- 1 tsp. vanilla extract

(For the vanilla cream and strawberry filling)

- 8 Tbsp. (½ cup) strawberry preserves
- 8 fl. oz. (1 cup) heavy whipping cream
- 1 Tbsp. vanilla extract
- 2 Tbsp. fine granulated sugar
- 3 Tbsp. powdered sugar (to lightly sieve on top)

How to make them:

1. Preheat the oven to 375° F then line your cupcake pans with 24 paper cups.
2. Cream the margarine and sugar in a bowl until they are light and fluffy, incorporating plenty of air.
3. Add the beaten eggs into the bowl 1 Tbsp. at a time, placing 1 tsp. of flour after each egg addition to avoid curdling the mixture.
4. Gently fold the remaining flour and baking powder into the mixture with a large spatula to incorporate as much air as possible.
5. Spoon the mixture evenly into prepared cups and bake for 15–20 minutes or until they have risen well and are a light golden color (a skewer should come out clean when inserted into the center of the cupcake).
6. Allow them to cool in pans for 5 minutes, then remove the cupcakes from tin and cool on a wire wrack.
7. When cupcakes have completely cooled, use a sharp serrated knife to cut a circle from the center of each one, forming a shallow cone, and set aside.
8. To make filling, beat the cream with an electric mixer and fold in the fine granulated sugar and vanilla.
9. To assemble the butterfly cupcakes, fill each hollow with 1 tsp. of strawberry preserves and top with 1 Tbsp. of fresh whipped vanilla cream (which can also be piped with piping bag).
10. Cut the reserved cones in half to form a semicircle and arrange the halves facing opposite directions to resemble butterfly wings.
11. Use a sieve to lightly sprinkle the tops with a little powdered sugar.

Pork and flame on the grill

Barbequed lamb and fresh Georgia peach salsa

the Southern GRILL

Southern barbeque, a long standing and very delicious part of the culture. Much debated, much admired & much enjoyed!

Outdoor fun, grilling in the South

Fire up the grill and have some fun in the summer months!

As I mentioned in earlier chapters, I grew up on a farm in Northern Ireland where my father raised sheep and cattle for the meat market. My uncles owned a cattle mart and abattoir, and my entire family has been heavily invested in the Irish meat industry for generations. It will stand to reason, then, when I tell you that my family and I loved to prepare and eat good meats. Generally speaking, people in Northern Ireland love their meats also, and as a testament we have a very fine livestock industry with quality produce and family butcher shops throughout the province that specialize in all kinds of prepared meats, from delicious sausages to succulent sirloins, each one perfect for back garden barbequing. We lacked only one thing: suitable weather.

In the summer months in Northern Ireland, any glint of sunlight will send very pale people scurrying into the garage to dig out "the barbecue," which will then be ceremoniously dusted off and set in place for outdoor grilling between intermittent rain showers. In Ireland we love to grill meats outdoors, but the weather is our biggest hindrance. It was an interesting experience, then, to move to the Deep South, where outdoor grilling has become a way of life. This time the weather, instead of being a hindrance, is a motivation. In hot Georgia summers, we discovered that one of the reasons people like to grill outdoors on back decks is to remove the primary cooking heat source out of their homes. After all, if you're paying to keep your home cool, why heat it up again with the oven and stovetop? Apart from that practicality, though, we fell in love with the Southern barbeque for tasty reasons. In other words, it's just finger-lickin' good!

So where did this meat-cooking culture in the South come from? For those early Scots-Irish immigrants, the harsh Ireland they left behind was one where meat was scarce. Most people ate root vegetables and drank buttermilk, but in the New World, game was plentiful and raising stock was possible given the much larger parcels of land they were carving out for themselves. So these settlers to the South had the good fortune of adapting to the more abundant meat sources around them and needed to improvise with cooking methods. These factors in no small way added to the folklore of Southern barbeque.

In those early days in the South, the simplest way (and some would argue the best way) to cook large quantities of meat was the now infamous pit barbeque. This method simply involved digging a large pit six feet across and four feet deep, filling the base with rocks, then adding a layer of fragrant wood such as hickory, which was abundant in the South, to burn off. Whole skinned deer or pigs or sheep were then lowered into the pit on spits and the pit was controlled to achieve a relatively low and consistent heat. The fat dripping from the meat then ensured the wonderful smoky results. Even though many real pit barbeque experiences can still be had across the South, most people do not grill in this way anymore but use gas or charcoal grills and smokers to achieve the desired result, which in most cases is still wonderful if cooked correctly.

In this chapter I will honor this wonderful culture found in the South and will take my own Irish spin on some of those fabled barbeque offerings. I'll be presenting several types of dishes that I feel are necessary to really do a backyard cookout justice, all with a distinctly Irish twist—from lamb with peach salsa, to sweet potato casserole, to a wonderfully tasty potato salad, to my special pork loin served with my own whiskey-fueled barbeque sauce! I have even included a fried chicken recipe in here, graciously given to me by one of my Southern chef pals that will keep your friends coming back for more. So fire up the barbeque, put your favorite beverages on ice and let's have some fun grilling Southern style!

Barbequed Lamb with a Georgia Peach Salsa
served with an olive oil mint drizzle

The Story:

As a farmhouse cook, my mother always insisted on making fresh mint sauce to accompany a leg of lamb for Sunday lunches, and in my experience, the fresh infused mint sauce was the perfect partner to the roast lamb. Here in Georgia, though, it is not always suitable to spend hours in a hot kitchen in summertime, so I have converted my Irish comfort food favorite into a barbeque delight that will impress your friends at cookouts on those hot summer days. The light and crunchy salsa is flavored with Georgia peaches for that Southern flair, and the entire ensemble works very well together.

Lamb ingredients (serves 6–8 people):
- 4–6 lbs. boneless leg of lamb (cut into 8 pieces)

Marinade ingredients:
- 6 fl. oz. (¾ cup) natural yogurt
- 2 fl. oz. (¼ cup) Dijon mustard
- juice and zest of 1 lime
- 2 rosemary sprigs (stems removed)
- 2 cloves of garlic
- ½ Vidalia onion
- 1" piece of root ginger (peeled)
- 1 medium red chili pepper (seeds removed)
- 1 tsp. kosher salt
- ½ tsp. ground black pepper

Mint drizzle ingredients:
- Bunch of mint (1½ cups with the stems removed)
- 2 tsp. sugar
- ½ tsp. kosher salt
- 3 Tbsp. white balsamic vinegar
- 4 fl. oz. (½ cup) olive oil

Peach salsa ingredients:
- 4 peaches (peeled, stoned, and finely chopped)
- 1 medium tomato (core removed, peeled, and finely chopped)
- 1 small red onion (chopped)
- 1 vine sweet mini red chili pepper (seeds removed and finely chopped)
- 1 jalapeño pepper (seeds removed and finely chopped)
- 4 Tbsp. cilantro (stems removed and chopped)
- juice of one lime
- ¼ tsp. kosher salt and several grinds of black pepper
- ¼ tsp. sugar

How to make it:

1. In a food processor or blender mix all the marinade ingredients together to make a smooth paste.
2. Rub the resulting paste all over the cut portions of the lamb and marinade for 4–6 hours or overnight, covered in the refrigerator.
3. Preheat the grill to a high heat.
4. Remove the meat from the marinade and discard the remaining liquid.
5. Place the lamb on the grill and cook on both sides for the first few minutes to sear.
6. Turn the heat down to medium and continue to cook the lamb according to your preference, turning frequently. (The lamb is cooked medium to well after 30–40 minutes.)
7. While the lamb is cooking on the grill, prepare the mint drizzle by placing the mint leaves, sugar, vinegar and salt in a food processor. Pulse in the processor for a few seconds to form a roughly chopped paste, and then slowly blend in the olive oil.
8. Transfer the resulting liquid in to a small bowls and then set aside.
9. Make the salsa by chopping and combining all the salsa ingredients into a medium-sized bowl. Refrigerate until ready to serve.
10. When the lamb is cooked according to taste, remove from the grill and let it rest for 10 minutes to allow the juices to settle.
11. To serve, place the lamb in the center of each serving plate then drizzle a little mint dressing onto the plate and spoon some over the meat.
12. Spoon some salsa onto the side of the plate and garnish with a sprig of mint.

Arugula Citrus Salad
with red onions, brown sugar-cinnamon-soda bread croutons, and an orange champagne and white truffle oil vinaigrette

the story:

This wonderful summer salad is one of my favorites for company and Southern firefly picnics. Arugula (also known as "Rocket" in the UK and Ireland) has a pepper-like flavor, and when paired with citrus, compliments smoked meats without taking away from the true barbeque flavors. Rocket salads, or Arugula salads, are very popular in Northern Ireland during the summer, but for this recipe I've added a superb *fusion* touch by including some brown sugar-cinnamon-soda bread croutons to the mix. Irish, yet American, yet Southern, yet not. A bit of everything and one of my best salads I think!

Arugula citrus salad ingredients (serves 4):

- 6 large handfuls of Arugula, or rocket salad greens
- 4 blood oranges (skin removed and split into segments)
- ¼ red onion (very thinly sliced)

Cinnamon croutons ingredients:

- 4 slices of plain Irish soda bread (cut in 1" thick slices)
- 2 Tbsp. butter (melted)
- 3 Tbsp. brown sugar
- 1 tsp. cinnamon
- ¼ tsp. nutmeg
- pinch of kosher salt

Vinaigrette ingredients:

- 2 fl. oz. (¼ cup) champagne vinegar
- 1 shallot (minced)
- 2 Tbsp. orange juice
- zest of one orange
- ½ tsp. celery seed salt
- several turns of milled black pepper
- 2 Tbsp. honey
- 6 Tbsp. canola oil
- 2 Tbsp. white truffle oil

How to make it:

1. To make the croutons, first preheat your oven to 400° F.
2. Combine the sugar, cinnamon, and nutmeg in a small bowl.
3. Cube the bread and toss the bread chunks into melted butter.
4. Place the bread chunks on a large baking pan and sprinkle over the sugar and cinnamon mixture.
5. Bake for 6–8 minutes or until crispy. Shake the pan and turn the croutons halfway through baking time for an even result.
6. Prepare the vinaigrette in processor by mincing the shallots, champagne vinegar, orange juice, orange zest, celery seed salt, pepper, and honey together.
7. Add the canola oil and white truffle oil in a slow drizzle as the vinaigrette is mixing, then set aside.
8. To prepare the oranges, cut off the top and the base of the oranges. Stand each piece of fruit upright and cut off the peel and pith with a large serrated knife.
9. Using a sharp knife, slice the fruit from the top of the base right around to the sides, following the natural curve and the individual segments of the fruit.
10. Just before serving, season the Arugula with a little salt and pepper, tossing it for evenness, then add the croutons, oranges, red onions, and vinaigrette.
11. Serve right away.

Deep South Sweet Potato Casserole

the story:

The first time I experienced eating sweet potato casserole was at my friend's grandmother's home, a lady with the Scots-Irish name of McCall who lived on a watermelon farm in Mississippi. I will never forget her warm hospitality when we sat at her dinner table eating a slowly cooked beef pot roast, freshly picked green beans and her famous sweet potato casserole. It felt like *going home* and ever since I can not imagine a Thanksgiving or Christmas dinner without this superb Southern side dish.

Sweet potato ingredients (serves 4):

- 6 medium size sweet potatoes
- 4 oz. (½ cup) sugar
- ¼ tsp. salt
- 4 oz. (½ cup butter)
- 1 tsp. vanilla
- 4 Tbsp. whole milk
- 1 egg (beaten)

(For the Topping)

- 4 oz. (½ cup) brown sugar
- 2 Tbsp. butter (melted)
- 2 oz. (½ cup) pecans (chopped)
- ½ tsp. cinnamon

How to make it:

1. Place the sweet potatoes in a pan of cold water and bring to a boil. Cover and reduce heat to medium low and cook for abut 30–35 minutes until tender. Cool slightly and peel the potatoes. Mash with a potato masher until smooth.
2. Combine the cooked sweet potatoes, sugar, salt, melted butter, egg and milk and beat until smooth.
3. Grease a 9x9" pan and arrange the potato mixture in the dish.
4. Combine brown sugar cinnamon, butter and chopped pecans in a bowl and sprinkle on top of the potatoes in the dish.
5. Bake for about 30 minutes or until *bubbly* and brown.

southern summer steak and sweet onions

The Story:

The best of Southern summer entertaining is this simple but flavorful duo of steak with sweet Vidalia onions. These famous onions hail from the city of Vidalia in South Georgia and are a famously sweet and flavorful onion that seems destined to enhance any Southern summer cookout. Learning from established Southern cooks, I create my "sweet onion parcels" on the grill with some foil and beef bouillon, making the most delicious partner to the flavorful flank steak. Serve up with some crusty bread for a ton of Southern summer flavor!

Georgia summer steak ingredients:
- 2 lbs. flank or hanger steak

Steak marinade ingredients (makes ¼ cup):
- 1 tsp. coarse sea salt
- ½ tsp. freshly ground black pepper
- 1 tsp. cayenne pepper
- 1 tsp. cumin
- 1 Tbsp. brown sugar
- 2 fl. oz. (¼ cup) pineapple juice
- 1 Tbsp. soy sauce
- 2 cloves garlic (crushed)
- 1 tsp. Worcestershire sauce

Vidalia onion parcel ingredients:
- 2 medium Vidalia or other sweet variety onions
- 1 beef stock cube
- 2 Tbsp. unsalted butter
- pinch of ground black pepper
- heavy-duty aluminum foil

How to make it:

1. Combine the marinade ingredients together in a bowl and pour them into a large resealable plastic bag.
2. Add the steak to the bag and marinate for 8–24 hours, or overnight in the refrigerator.
3. Preheat your grill to hot.
4. Begin to prepare the onions by cutting 4 pieces of aluminum into squares that you will use to wrap onion parcels.
5. Peel the onions carefully, still keeping the root in tact.
6. Slice off the top of the onion using a sharp knife and cut just enough from the root for onion to sit flat.
7. Use a knife to dig and gently cut a cone shape in the center of onion and then slice diagonally into six pieces.
8. Place ½ beef stock cube in each onion center, along with 1 Tbsp. butter.
9. Sprinkle a little ground black pepper over them and place each onion into the center of the prepared foil. Wrap up tightly.
10. Place the onion parcels on grill and cook for 15 minutes before adding the steaks, with total cooking time being 30 minutes.
11. Remove the steak from the marinade, discarding the liquid, and place them on a hot grill that is lightly brushed with vegetable oil.
12. Sear on high heat, then turn the heat down and continue to grill for 6–7 minutes on each side for *medium*.
13. Remove the steak and onions from the grill and allow the steak to rest for 5 minutes.
14. Slice the steak diagonally across the grain.
15. Open up the onion parcels and slice the onions, reserving all the liquid.
16. To serve, arrange the sliced steak on a platter or a plate and top with the Vidalia onion. Spoon the reserved juice from the onions over the meat and platter.

Loin Pork Chop with Irish Whiskey BBQ Sauce
served with an avocado and corn relish

The Story:

Good barbeque in the South is almost a religion, with strong opinions abounding about dry rubs, marinating, and *of course,* having the *perfect* barbeque sauce. In Georgia, barbeque sauce is red, sweet, and spicy; in South Carolina, barbeque sauce is a yellow, mustard-based variety, while in Kentucky, they are famous for their *bourbon* sauce. Each region seems to have its own special variety, and now I'm creating yet another! My *Shamrock & Peach* sauce is naturally influenced by my journey from Ireland to Georgia, and I have a few special ingredients of my own to add, including some great Irish whiskey!

Sweet pork dry rub ingredients:

- 2 Tbsp. brown sugar
- 1 Tbsp. kosher salt
- 1 tsp. ground black pepper
- 1 Tbsp. ground cumin
- 1½ Tbsp. cayenne pepper
- 1 tsp. garlic powder
- 1 tsp. cinnamon
- ½ tsp. nutmeg
- 6 loin pork chops (rib in)

Irish whiskey barbeque sauce ingredients:

- 2 Tbsp. butter
- ¼ large onion (chopped)
- 2 cloves garlic (crushed)
- 8 fl. oz. (1 cup) Irish whiskey
- 8 fl. oz. (1 cup) ketchup
- 6 fl. oz. (¾ cup) apple cider vinegar
- 2 fl. oz. (¼ cup) water
- 6 Tbsp. cup brown sugar
- 3 Tbsp. Worcestershire sauce
- 1 tsp. kosher salt
- ¼ tsp. freshly ground black pepper
- 1 tsp. cayenne pepper
- 2 tsp. cocoa powder
- ¾ tsp. cumin

Avocado and corn relish ingredients:

- 1 cup corn (about 3 ears of corn husked)
- 1 Tbsp. olive oil
- 1 small red pepper (cored, seeded, and finely diced)
- 1 small hot green chili pepper (1 Tbsp. finely chopped)
- 2 medium avocados (peeled, stoned, and finely chopped)
- 2 Tbsp. lime juice
- 2 Tbsp. cilantro (chopped)
- ¼ onion (chopped)
- 1 small garlic clove (minced)
- ½ tsp. sea salt

How to make it:

1. Combine all the dry ingredients to make the rub.
2. Apply the dry rub to the surface of the uncooked pork chops before grilling. This can be done several hours in advance or just before grilling.
3. To make the barbeque sauce, melt the butter in a small saucepan and cook the onion for a few minutes until they are soft but not browned. Add the garlic and cook for 1 minute more. Then combine *all* the remaining ingredients and simmer gently for 20–25 minutes or until the sauce has been *slightly* reduced. Cool slightly before processing with an electric blender until smooth.
4. Preheat your grill to high.
5. While grill is heating, prepare the *avocado corn relish.*
6. To do so, remove the corn from the husk and sauté in a large pan with olive oil for 4–5 minutes. When done, set aside and allow the cooked corn to cool.
7. Place the pork chops on the hot grill and cook on each side for 2 minutes to sear meat. Reduce heat to medium and cook for a further 5–8 minutes on each side. *(To check that pork is cooked, use a sharp knife to cut the thickest part of the chop and check that it is done to your preference.)*
8. Brush a little barbeque sauce over both sides of chops and cook for 1 more minute on each side.
9. Remove the meat from the grill and let rest for 5 minutes before serving.
10. Finish preparing the relish by adding the remaining ingredients to the corn and mix together.
11. To serve, brush the pork chops with a little more barbeque sauce and place chop on the center of the plate with a spoonful of avocado corn relish on top and to the side.

Golden Pear & Irish Blue Cheese Salad
with blackberry balsamic vinaigrette and spiced walnuts

The Story:

Blackberries grow wild in the hedgerows that line the country lanes and byways throughout rural Northern Ireland, and the country road that led to our farm was no exception. In the summertime, the hedges are thick with fruit, and I have vivid memories of picking these lush purple berries as a child, staining my fingers black and blue in the process.

In this recipe I pair a blackberry dressing with pungent blue cheese, and the result tastes like the last of the Southern summer wine. Top with some ripe pear and you'll have a winning combination.

Salad ingredients (serves 4):
- 4 handfuls of salad greens (washed)
- 2 ripe pears (quartered and cored)
- handful of blackberries
- handful of spiced walnuts
- 4 oz. Irish blue cheese
- 2 fl. oz. (¼ cup) blackberry vinaigrette

Spiced walnuts ingredients:
- 12 oz. (2½ cups) walnuts
- 1 egg white
- 1 tsp. fine sea salt
- 2 Tbsp. sugar
- 1 tsp. cinnamon
- ¼ tsp. ginger
- ¼ tsp. nutmeg
- ¼ tsp. cayenne pepper

Blackberry vinaigrette ingredients:
- 5 oz. (1 cup) ripe blackberries
- juice of 1 lemon
- 2 fl. oz. (¼ cup) honey
- 1 shallot (minced)
- 2 fl. oz. (¼ cup) balsamic vinegar
- 6 fl. oz. (¾ cup) olive oil
- sea salt and pepper

How to make it:
1. Preheat the oven to 350° F.
2. To make the spiced walnuts, combine the sugar, salt, cinnamon, and cayenne in a bowl.
3. Coat the walnuts in egg white and toss them in the prepared dry mixture.
4. Spread the coated walnuts on a parchment-lined baking sheet and bake for 5 minutes.
5. Stir the nuts and bake for a further 5 minutes, being careful not to burn.
6. Prepare the vinaigrette by blending the blackberries and lemon juice in the food processor.
7. Strain to remove seeds.
8. Blend strained lemon blackberry purée, shallot, honey, and balsamic vinegar in the processor. Add the oil in a slow, steady drizzle.
9. Season with salt and pepper then refrigerate.
10. To serve, divide the salad mixture between 6 plates, then arrange the pears, blackberries, blue cheese, and a few spiced walnuts on top of each salad mixture.
11. Drizzle the dressing over the salad and serve.

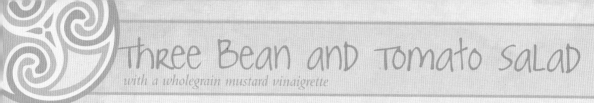

Three Bean and Tomato Salad
with a wholegrain mustard vinaigrette

The Story:

Just as it does in Ireland, the farmer's market scene continues to flourish in the South as people are increasingly concerned with processed foods, and there is nothing like bringing home a basket of locally grown young green beans and tomatoes to inspire you in the kitchen.

To prepare this healthy cookout salad and side dish, I use the freshest ingredients I can find and add some high-fiber soy and red kidney beans to the mix to make a delightfully colorful and flavorful salad, the perfect accompaniment to a cookout or to use as a vegetarian option.

Three Bean and tomato salad ingredients (serves 4–6):

(For the salad)

- 1 lb. green beans (ends trimmed)
- 12 oz. shelled soybeans (edamame)
- one 15-oz. can of red kidney beans (drained)
- 2 Tbsp. cilantro (chopped)
- 1 Tbsp. chives (chopped)
- ½ lb. tomatoes (cored & chopped)

(For the wholegrain mustard vinaigrette)

- 2 Tbsp. tarragon vinegar
- 1 Tbsp. whole grain mustard
- 2 tsp. honey
- 1 shallot (finely chopped)
- ½ tsp. kosher salt
- 1/8 tsp. ground black pepper
- 6 Tbsp. vegetable oil

How to make it:

1. To make the vinaigrette, combine the vinegar, mustard, honey, shallot, and seasoning in a food processor. Slowly drizzle in the oil as it mixes, then refrigerate when done.
2. To prepare the green beans, bring a small amount of water to a boil in a large saucepan, add the green beans, and cook uncovered for no more than 3 minutes, keeping them crisp and tender.
3. Drain and plunge the beans into a basin of ice water to stop the cooking process.
4. To prepare soy beans, bring 4 cups water to a boil; add the soybeans and ½ tsp. salt then boil for 5 minutes. Drain and cool.
5. Combine the green beans, soy beans, red kidney beans, cilantro, tomatoes, and dill together in a bowl.
6. Toss the resulting bean salad in vinaigrette and refrigerate.

Irish Potato and Vidalia Onion Bake
a Celtic-Southern fusion potato-au-gratin

The Story:

Almost every Irish meal includes the famous potato somewhere, and when a favorite Irish potato dish is fused with a wonderful native Georgia-grown sweet onion, it makes it a great thing indeed. The particular soil properties found in South Georgia produce that unique and flavorful onion, taking its name from the city of its origin, Vidalia, Georgia, and it is one of my Southern favorites! Some may also refer to this dish as *potato-au-gratin*, and it has become a requested favorite of mine over the years. I think the flavor of the potatoes and sweet onions, kissed with garlic and combined with the cream and cheese, make an irresistible winner indeed!

Potato and onion ingredients:

- 1½ lbs. (5 medium Yukon gold variety potatoes)
- 1 Tbsp. butter (melted)
- 1 large garlic clove (cut in half)
- ½ large Vidalia or other sweet onion (thinly sliced)
- 12 fl. oz. (1½ cups) heavy whipping cream
- 2 fl. oz. (¼ cup) chicken stock
- kosher salt and freshly ground pepper
- 5 oz. (1¼ cups) mature white cheddar

How to make it:

1. Preheat the oven to 350° F.
2. Peel the potatoes and slice them as thinly as possible with a sharp paring knife.
3. Peel the onion, cut it in half, then slice into long, thin strips.
4. Grease the casserole dish with the melted butter.
5. Crush a garlic clove with a knife and smear it around the inside of the casserole dish to introduce a subtle flavor without overpowering the dish.
6. Discard the spent garlic clove and arrange the sliced potatoes in rows inside the casserole dish. Layer the onions in between the layers of potato and continue until all the sliced potatoes and onions are in the dish.
7. Mix the cream and stock together in a jug and pour over the potatoes.
8. Season the casserole with a little kosher salt and freshly ground pepper.
9. Bake for about 45 minutes or until potatoes are soft when pierced with a fork and top is bubbling all over.
10. While casserole is baking, grate your cheese and set aside.
11. Remove the dish from the oven and sprinkle with the grated cheese. Bake for a further 5–7 minutes until the cheese has melted and is golden brown on top.

Ford's Southern Farmstead Fried Chicken

The Story:

My friend Ford Fry is an extraordinary chef who has a flair for making the most wonderful Southern food. He has taken farmstead style of cooking to a new level here in Atlanta and has graciously shared with me his famous *JCT Southern Fried Chicken* recipe. This delicious and wonderfully moist fried chicken takes a little planning and time to prepare, but it's worth it to get a dish that will have your guests sucking on the bones and licking their fingers to no end! Not strictly a "grill dish," I know, but fried chicken is a Southern cookout tradition, and I just couldn't leave it out!

Southern fried chicken ingredients (makes 16 pieces):

- 2 whole organic 3–3.5 lb. chicken (each cut into 8 pieces)

(For the brine)

- 8 pints (1 gallon) water
- 8 oz. (1 cup) kosher salt
- 2 oz. (¼ cup) sugar
- 1 bay leaf
- 1 Tbsp. black peppercorns
- 1 bunch of fresh thyme

Second soak

- 1½ pints (3 cups) buttermilk

(For the seasoned flour)

- 16 oz. (4 cups) flour
- 4 oz. (1 cup) cornstarch
- 2 Tbsp. kosher salt
- 2 Tbsp. black pepper
- 2 Tbsp. granulated garlic
- 1 Tbsp. cayenne pepper
- 2 tsp. ground nutmeg

(For the fry)

- canola oil for frying

How to make it:

Day one:

1. Using an appropriate sized pot, place all 6 ingredients of the brine together and bring to a boil.
2. Turn off the heat and let the liquid cool to room temperature.
3. Place the chicken pieces into a large sealable bowl or container, completely cover with the room temperature brine, and place in the refrigerator for 24 hours.

Day two:

1. Once the chicken has brined, strain off all the brine liquid and discard the herbs.
2. Cover chicken with buttermilk and return to the refrigerator until you are ready to fry.

Frying:

1. Using a large cast iron skillet and a deep fat thermometer, fill the skillet halfway with canola oil then heat the oil to 300° F. (The oil temperature should fluctuate between 280–300°.)
2. Once oil is stable, drain off the buttermilk from the bowl and dredge the chicken pieces into the seasoned flour. Pat off any excess and carefully place into the hot oil. Repeat with all the remaining chicken pieces.
3. Once the chicken becomes golden brown on one side (roughly 10 minutes), turn over and brown on the other side. *(To be safe, place a meat thermometer into the chicken closest to the center and next to the bone. The temperature should read no less than 160°.)*
4. Remove the chicken from the oil and rest the pieces on a rack-lined tray, allowing them to drain.
5. If you will be making chicken in batches, feel free to hold the completed chicken pieces in a 200° oven until you are ready to serve.
6. Sprinkle with herbs and serve right away!

Glover Park, Marietta Georgia

Pink Georgia Dogwoods in bloom

the Southern sweet

Sugar icing, chocolate indulgence, fresh cream, caramel and all things we love about the Southern sweet table, arranged for your delight and pure enjoyment!

Bullock Hall, Roswell, Georgia

The Southern sweet table, a love affair with sugar

The Southern Sweet: A Love Affair with Sugar

After moving to Georgia, it didn't take us long to realize the incredible love affair that Southerners have with sugar, pies, and puddings. I thought the Scots-Irish were bad, considering our chocolate-infused obsessions with dessert, but could not imagine just what a big slice of the food culture *sweets* occupy in the South. When invited to any cookout, barbeque, or party in Atlanta, we would instinctively know that the sweet selection after the main course would be extensive and interesting, to say the least—so much so that at many gatherings we assume that the main course is *not* the chicken or the beef but the pies, cakes, and cookies that will surely follow. To showcase this, it is quite normal at any Southern party to have the range of sweets offered displayed on elaborate cake stands and platters on a separate table or sideboard and adorned on crisp white linen with fresh flowers to boot. Guests arriving at the party will invariably peruse the sweets and ponder on the moistness of sugar-infused creations on offer and will talk up those sweets from arrival to exit.

It seems that most Southern families have secret recipes for cupcakes or a family recipe for a pie invented by a remote ancestor, and if you enjoy the sweet upon offer, a story of its origins will surely follow. We love this, and it's so Celtic in culture to brag about cherished relatives and family secrets, especially to new friends or total strangers. This much we have learned: if you want to impress in the South, arrive at the party with the best dessert or pie possible and everyone will love you for it, but be prepared to follow the applause with the history of the creation or you might just miss the boat!

As another case in point in regard to this Southern love affair, my husband and I recently spent an afternoon in the historic Marietta Square, a quaint and very Southern district in the suburbs of Atlanta, and counted no less than seven sweet or pie specialty shops around us offering a bewildering range of everything from traditional pecan and key lime pies to homemade ice creams and fresh cookies. Perhaps the pastry store is to small Southern towns what the pub is to Ireland, an essential part of the culture!

I suppose history also plays a large part in this love affair with sugar, as the old Southern states grew sugar on plantations and used sugar in days gone by to cure and preserve foods. Think of sugar-cured hams or bacon or cakes covered in boiled sugar and you'll get the idea. As the Irish were using it in their tea, their cousins in the South were using it in everything!

The link between the Scots-Irish and the Southern sweet obsession is an interesting one that has many parallels when considering the two cultures. In Northern Ireland and Scotland we just love our sweet things, whether they are boiled, cooked, or fried, and in many ways they are a comfort food on long, dark evenings. This culture has spilled over to the South, but given the warmer climate and differing growing conditions, the choice of sweet things on offer in the Southern states is invariably longer. In Georgia, pecans, peanuts, peaches, and other tree-borne goodies form a large part of the ingredient offerings, taking the place of the rhubarb, blackberries, and gooseberries that were common in the gardens and hedgerows of Ireland. And for me as a cook, it has been so interesting learning about these new ingredients and creating new recipes to include them in. I've had so much fun reinventing old Irish sweet recipes with new Southern ingredients and seeing them come to life in interesting ways.

These past few years, several of my Southern girlfriends have helped me in this odyssey as we've swapped ideas and recipes for tea parties and goodies that I've come to cherish over time. I am now glad to share some of those treasures with you in the pages of this book. These pies, cakes, cupcakes, and creations form some of my favorite moments in a wonderful journey of discovery as I too join the bandwagon on this Southern sugar love affair.

oatmeal & sea salt caramel cupcakes

oatmeal cupcakes with a cream cheese frosting and sea salt caramel drizzle

the story:

One of my dear Southern friends shared a recipe with me for oatmeal cakes from an old Appalachian church cookbook she had, and it was an inspiration. From that old recipe, which seemed very *Old World* Scots-Irish to me, I created this new recipe for cupcakes, using Irish oatmeal. I also gave it a modern twist with some whipped cream cheese frosting and a delicious sea salt caramel drizzle on top. The combination of flavors works wonderfully, and after tasting one cupcake you will definitely be hooked!

Oatmeal cupcake ingredients (makes 2 dozen cupcakes):

- 10 fl. oz. (1¼ cup) boiling water
- 6 oz. (1 cup) Irish oats
- 4 oz. (½ cup) butter (room temperature)
- 8 oz. (1 cup) brown sugar
- 8 oz. (1 cup) white sugar
- 2 eggs (room temperature)
- 1 tsp. vanilla
- 6 oz. (1½ cups) flour (sifted)
- 1 tsp. baking soda
- ½ tsp. cinnamon
- 1/8 tsp. nutmeg
- ½ tsp. salt

Cream cheese frosting ingredients:

- 8-oz. package cream cheese (room temperature)
- 4 oz. (½ cup) unsalted butter
- 1 Tbsp. sea salt caramel sauce
- 1 lb. powdered sugar

Sea salt caramel sauce ingredients:

- 4 oz. (½ cup) granulated sugar
- 4 fl. oz. (½ cup) heavy whipping cream
- ½ tsp. coarse kosher salt
- 3 Tbsp unsalted butter

How to make them:

1. Begin by putting 24 paper baking cups in a muffin pan.
2. Pour boiling water over the Irish oats and soak for 20 minutes.
3. Preheat your oven to 350° F.
4. Cream the butter using an electric mixer, then add the sugars and beat until well combined.
5. Add the eggs to the mixture one at a time, beating for 1 minute after each addition.
6. Add the oats and vanilla, then mix well.
7. Sift the flour, soda, salt, cinnamon, and nutmeg and fold into the cake mixture.
8. Spoon the resulting batter into the baking cups.
9. Bake the cupcakes for 15–20 minutes until well risen and firm to the touch.
10. Transfer the cupcakes to a wire rack to cool.
11. To make sea salt caramel sauce, slowly melt the sugar in a small saucepan, stirring all the time until it melts and caramelizes.
12. Remove from heat and allow to cool slightly before beating in butter, 1 Tbsp. at a time.
13. Beat in the cream and salt and stir to thicken. Allow to cool.
14. To make the frosting, beat together the butter and cream cheese. Add the powdered sugar and sea salted caramel. Beat until fluffy and smooth.
15. To assemble cupcakes, pipe the butter cream on top of each cupcake using a star-shaped nozzle then drizzle a little of the sea salt caramel on top of each one.

Atlanta Milk Chocolate Coca-Cola Cake
with an Irish cream filling

the story:

Cola cake is another one of those really fun recipes found all over the South in church cookbooks and scribbled on homemade recipe note cards tucked away in drawers. Two worlds collide in this *Shamrock & Peach* version as we combine Ireland's favorite liqueur with Atlanta's famous beverage.

Cola cake ingredients:

- 8½ oz. (2 cups) all-purpose flour (sifted)
- 1 tsp. baking soda
- ½ tsp. salt
- 3 Tbsp. cocoa powder
- 8 oz. (1 cup) butter
- 14 oz. (2 cups) sugar
- 8 fl. oz. (1 cup) Coca-Cola
- 1 tsp. vanilla
- 2 eggs (beaten)
- 4 fl. oz. (½ cup) buttermilk

Cola frosting ingredients:

- 11.5 oz. (2 cups) quality milk chocolate
- 4 oz. (½ cup) butter
- 4 fl. oz. (½ cup) Coke
- 1 lb. powdered sugar
- chocolate shavings (to garnish)

Irish cream filling ingredients:

- 7 oz. (1¾ cup) powdered sugar
- 3 oz. Irish butter (softened)
- 2 fl. oz. (¼ cup) Irish cream liqueur

How to make it:

1. Preheat the oven to 350° F.
2. Grease and line two 9" round layer cake pans with parchment paper.
3. Sieve the flour, salt, baking soda, and cocoa powder together and set aside.
4. Cream the butter and sugar together in an electric mixer until light and fluffy.
5. Add the eggs 1 Tbsp. at a time, alternating with a tablespoon of the flour while scraping down the sides of the bowl to make a smooth, even batter.
6. Combine the buttermilk, cola and vanilla. Slowly beat in the remaining dry ingredients, alternating this time with the wet ingredients, beating after each addition to distribute all the ingredients evenly.
7. Divide the batter equally into baking pans and bake the cakes for 30 minutes or until the center of the cake comes out clean when inserted with a skewer.
8. Let the cakes rest in pans for 10 minutes and then invert cakes onto a wire rack to cool. Garnish with chocolate shavings.
9. To make the Irish cream frosting filling, beat the butter in an electric mixer and *slowly* incorporate the powdered sugar and Irish cream liqueur until smooth.
10. To make the chocolate frosting, break up the chocolate bar into pieces and melt with butter in *a double boiler* on low heat, stirring until smooth.
11. Allow the chocolate mixture to cool slightly then transfer to an electric mixer, blending in the powdered sugar and cola. Beat until smooth.
12. To assemble the cake, place the cake, bottom side up, on a serving plate. Spoon the Irish cream liqueur frosting into the center on top and spread to edges. Top with the second cake layer and spread chocolate frosting around top and sides of cake.

Boozy Irish Whiskey Truffle Cheesecake
with Irish cream and a chocolate ganache

The Story:

This is a rather indulgent and super rich cheesecake but always a really popular dessert on my catering menu with the Ulster Kitchen, and once you read through the list of ingredients you will see why! The decadent and splendid combinations of Irish whiskey truffle cream with a chocolate ganache, cream are the stuff of legends. Bring this delight to any Southern backyard party or event and you will be the talk of the town and the envy of all!

Boozy Irish cheesecake ingredients:

(For the base)
- 8 oz. (2 cups) crushed digestive biscuit (or graham crackers)
- 4 oz. (½ cup) butter

(For the Irish whiskey truffle layer)
- 1 envelope unflavored gelatin (1.8 g)
- 4 oz. (½ cup) sugar
- ½ pint (1 cup) boiling water
- 24 oz. (4 cups) semi-sweet chocolate chips
- 4 oz. (½ cup) butter
- 1 lb. cream cheese (at room temperature)
- 4 Tbsp. (¼ cup) Irish whiskey

(For the Irish cream layer)
- 8 oz. cream cheese (at room temperature)
- 5½ oz. (1 cup) powdered sugar
- 6 fl. oz. (¾ cup) heavy whipping cream
- 2 Tbsp. Irish cream liquor

(For the chocolate ganache layer)
- 5 oz. (¾ cup) quality milk chocolate
- 2 fl. oz. (¼ cup) heavy whipping cream

How to make it:
1. Melt the butter and combine with the digestive biscuit cookie crumbs or graham cracker crumbs. Then press the mixture into the base of an 8" *spring form pan*.
2. Prepare Irish cream layer by beating the cream cheese with powdered sugar, then gradually add the heavy whipping cream and the Irish cream.
3. Pour filling on top of cookie base. Refrigerate while preparing chocolate truffle layer.
4. In a double boiler, melt the chocolate and butter over low heat. Allow to cool slightly.
5. Mix the gelatin and sugar together in a small bowl. Add the boiling water and stir for 5 minutes until the gelatin has completely dissolved.
6. Beat the cream cheese stopping to scrape down the sides of the bowl, and then slowly add the gelatin mixture, chocolate mixture and Irish whiskey.
7. Pour filling on top of Irish cream layer. Allow at least 2 hours for the cheesecake to set in the refrigerator.
8. Prepare the chocolate ganache layer by melting the chocolate and cream in a double boiler. Allow to cool slightly before pouring over cheesecake.
9. Refrigerate until ready to slice and serve.

Rhubarb & Peach Crumble with Fresh Ginger Cream

The Story:

In Northern Ireland cooking we love to combine fresh strawberries with rhubarb and find that the sweetness of the berries pairs well with the tartness of the rhubarb, which many people in Ulster grow in their back garden lots. But living in Georgia, also known as the Peach State, I have changed the recipe from strawberries to sweet Georgia peaches, finding that the peaches, when in season, are every bit as delicious. So this is a true fusion recipe, combining a very traditional Irish ingredient with a very traditional Georgia ingredient.

Ingredients:

(For the syrup and fruit)
- 8 oz. (1 cup) water
- 7 oz. (1 cup) granulated sugar
- 3 Tbsp. cornstarch
- 1 tsp. vanilla
- 2 large rhubarb stocks (4 cups) cut into ¼" slices
- 5 or 6 peaches (3 cups), skin removed and sliced

(For the crumble)
- 7 oz. (1 cup) old-fashioned oats
- 8 oz. (1 cup) brown sugar
- 4½ oz. (1 cup) flour
- 6 oz. (¾ cup) butter
- pinch of salt
- 1 tsp. cinnamon
- dash of nutmeg

Ginger fresh cream ingredients:
- 8 fl. oz. (1 cup) heavy whipping cream
- 2 Tbsp. super fine granulated sugar
- 1½ Tbsp. finely chopped crystallized ginger

How to make the crumble:

1. In a large mixing bowl add the oats, sugar, flour, salt, cinnamon, and nutmeg.
2. Add the diced butter and, using your fingertips, work the mixture until it resembles *coarse breadcrumbs*.
3. Lightly butter a 9x13" or equivalent pan and pour the peach and rhubarb mixture from above into the baking dish.
4. Sprinkle the crumb mixture *evenly* on top of the fruit.
5. Place the baking dish in the oven and bake for 45 minutes or until the filling is bubbly and the topping is golden brown.
6. Best served warm with a serving of ginger fresh cream.

How to make the syrup:

1. In a saucepan, whisk to combine the sugar, cornstarch, water, and vanilla.
2. Over a medium heat cook together until *clear* then set aside.
3. Preheat your oven to 350° F.
4. Combine the peaches and rhubarb together and toss in the prepared sugar syrup from step one.

How to make Ginger fresh cream:

1. Whisk the cream and sugar in a chilled mixing bowl until *soft peaks* appear.
2. Finely shred the crystallized ginger with a pairing knife or place in food processor to finely chop.
3. Fold the finely chopped ginger into the whipped fresh cream.
4. Refrigerate until ready to serve.

PaDDy's Chocolate Mint Pie with an orange Twist

The Story:

A green pie with an orange twist, now that is a fusion worth talking about for a Northern Irish girl! This was the first dessert I made for my husband when we were dating, so I had to include it in my book. A wonderfully light and not too sweet pie that combines the cool combination of mint and chocolate, always the best way to end a meal, and it looks great on the plate into the bargain! A great talking point for Saint Patrick's Day dinners or as a light dessert to end a summer time backyard cookout, you decide.

Crust ingredients:
- 1½ cups (6 oz.) graham cracker crumbs or digestive biscuits
- 1 Tbsp. coca powder
- 2 oz. butter (¼ cup butter)

Pie ingredients:
- 32 large marshmallows (8½ oz.)
- ½ cup (4 fl. oz.) whole milk
- 6 Tbsp. crème de menthe
- 2–3 drops of green food coloring
- 1½ cups (12 fl. oz.) heavy whipping cream

Orange chocolate sauce ingredients:
- one 8-oz. bar dark chocolate/orange flavor chocolate (broken into pieces)
- 6 fl. oz. (¾ cup) whipping cream

Garnish:
- sprigs of mint
- 1 orange (segmented)

How to make it:

1. To make the crust, crush the cookies in food processor and combine with melted butter and coca powder. Press into the bottom of 8" pie plate and bake for 10 minutes. Remove from oven and cool.
2. In a medium saucepan over low heat, melt the marshmallows in milk, stirring with a wooden spoon until they have melted. Allow to cool.
3. Next, stir in the crème de Menthe, then beat the heavy whipping cream until *soft peaks* appear and slowly fold in green marshmallow mixture.
4. Pour into the pie crust. Refrigerate.
5. To make orange chocolate sauce, melt the chocolate over a double boiler with the cream and stir until smooth.
6. To serve the pie, place the pie in center of the plate and garnish with a slice of segmented orange, a little orange zest, and a sprig of mint. Drizzle the plate with the chocolate orange sauce.

Rolled Pavlova with Meyer Lemon Curd

The Story:

Funny how a dessert that originated in New Zealand and is named after a Russian ballerina can be so popular in Ireland! Yet, go into any coffee shop in Belfast or anywhere else, and Pavlova is bound to be on the menu. The Irish love this wonderful dish, and it's easy to see why. When you bite into the crunchy sweet meringue, contrasted with the tart lemon curd, it is simply delectable. Pavlova is also beautifully light and makes a great mid-morning dessert; hence the popularity in coffee shops, no doubt. And now, you can make your very own version at home!

Pavlova ingredients:
- 4 large egg whites (room temperature)
- 6 oz. (¾ cup) fine granulated sugar
- 1 tsp. cornstarch (plus more for dusting on baking sheet)
- 1 tsp. white vinegar
- 1 tsp. clear vanilla extract

Filling ingredients:
- 2 fl. oz (¼ cup) Meyer lemon curd (recipe below)
- 6 fl. oz. (¾ cup) fresh whipped cream
- ½ tsp. powdered sugar (to sprinkle and serve)

Lemon curd ingredients:
- 4 Meyer lemons
- 5 eggs (beaten)
- 4 oz. (½ cup) butter
- 16 oz. (2 cups) granulated sugar

How to make the Pavlova:
1. Preheat the oven to 350°.
2. Prepare a 13¼x9¼" small cookie pan by greasing well and sprinkling a little cornstarch over wax paper.
3. Beat the egg whites in a bowl with an electric mixer until *soft peaks* appear.
4. Beat in the sugar, tbsp. at a time, until the meringue is thick and shiny. Finally, gently fold in the cornstarch, vinegar, and vanilla.
5. Carefully spread meringue over wax-papered pan and place in the oven.
6. Bake for about 12–15 minutes. Prepare a second sheet of wax paper and sprinkle with a little sugar and tip meringue out on top.
7. When meringue is cool, peal off the lining paper and spread over the lemon curd and fresh cream. Roll up the meringue and sprinkle with a little powdered sugar to serve.

How to make Lemon curd:
8. Zest the lemons and then extract the juice.
9. Bring about 1" of water to a boil in a medium saucepan then reduce heat to low and place a metal bowl on top to form a double boiler. Place butter in pan.
10. While butter is melting, finely whisk together eggs, sugar, lemon juice, and zest.
11. Combine all ingredients over a low heat and cook mixture, whisking occasionally for about 10 minutes. The curd will change color and be thickened enough to coat the back of a spoon when ready.
12. Strain mixture into a clean bowl. When I make this, I strain the curd twice. Let cool before filling in a jar.
13. Store for up to 2 weeks in the refrigerator.

Irish Tipsy Dark Chocolate Raspberry Trifles

The Story:

These wonderful chocolaty dessert treats are very easy to make and are a fun Irish spin on the traditional English sherry trifle, using Irish whiskey instead of sherry. Decadent, fun and delicious, the chocolate custard can be made days in advance and stored in the refrigerator with the top sealed with plastic wrap. Make as a large trifle to place on the table to share, or in individual glasses for a fun and elegant end to the meal.

Irish tipsy trifle ingredients (serves 4–6):

- 4 oz. lady fingers or an 8" sponge cake (cut into small pieces)
- 3 Tbsp. raspberry preserves
- 4 Tbsp. (¼ cup) raspberry-flavored liqueur
- 4 Tbsp. (¼ cup) whiskey
- 10 oz. raspberries
- 4 Tbsp. (¼ cup) sugar (plus 2 Tbsp. water)
- dark chocolate custard (see recipe below)
- 4 fl. oz. (½ cup) heavy whipping cream (1 cup whipped)
- 1 Tbsp. fine granulated sugar

(For the garnish)

- 3 oz. (¼ cup) chocolate (shaved)
- 6 mint sprigs
- 6 raspberries

Dark chocolate custard ingredients:

- 4 egg yolks
- 1 Tbsp. corn flour
- 8 fl. oz. (1 cup) whole milk
- 8 fl. oz. (1 cup) light cream
- 2 Tbsp. sugar
- 11.5 oz (1½ cups) dark organic chocolate (at least 70% cocoa)

How to make them:

1. Spread raspberry preserves over *lady fingers* or sponge cake and cut into small pieces.
2. Layer the sponge in the base of parfait glasses or one large bowl.
3. Sprinkle sugar over the raspberries and add a little water to make the syrup. Stir and set aside.
4. Combine whiskey and raspberry-flavored liqueur together and sprinkle over the sponge layer.
5. Spoon the raspberries with the syrup over the sponge.
6. Pour the prepared chocolate custard over the fruit and sponge base.
7. Whip the cream with granulated sugar. Spoon the cream on top of each trifle.
8. Garnish with a raspberry, chocolate shavings, and a sprig of fresh mint.

How to make the custard:

9. Gently heat the milk in a small saucepan, being careful not to boil. Remove from the heat.
10. In a clean bowl combine the egg yolks, cornstarch, and sugar and gently whisk together.
11. Whisk in the warm milk to egg mixture and then transfer all the combined ingredients to the small saucepan used to heat the milk earlier.
12. Cook the custard on medium–low heat for 2 minutes, stirring constantly until the custard is thick enough to coat the back of a spoon. Stir in the chocolate until it has melted.

white chocolate and Irish Cream iced Parfaits

served on ginger snap cookies with a dark chocolate drizzle

The story:

This recipe was kindly shared with me by Chef Noel McMeel who is the Executive Head Chef at the prestigious Lough Erne golf resort situated in the scenic lakeland county of Fermanagh in Northern Ireland. I had the pleasure of meeting Noel in New York as one of the Irish chefs invited to represent the very best of the new culinary brilliance that is abundant throughout Ireland today. This recipe is a light, delicate and sophisticated ending to a great meal combining two ingredients that are a match made in heaven, namely white chocolate and Irish cream liqueur tied with some delicate ginger snap cookies. Who could possibly resist?

Chef Noel McMeel

White chocolate ice parfait ingredients (makes 12):

- 11 oz. (1 1/3 cup) granulated sugar
- 2½ fl. oz. (1/3 cup) water
- 7.2 oz. (about 7) egg yolks
- 15 fl. oz. (just under 2 cups) heavy whipping cream
- 2 fl. oz. (1/4 cup) Irish Cream liqueur
- 8 oz. white chocolate (1 cup quality chips)

Ginger snap cookies ingredients:

- 2¼ oz. unsalted butter
- 4 oz. extra fine granulated sugar
- 1¼ fl. oz. (62.5 g) thick golden cane syrup
- 2¼ oz. all purpose flour (sifted)
- ½ tsp. powdered ginger (sifted)

Garnish ingredients:

- 4 oz. (½ cup) dark chocolate (melted)
- 4 fl. oz. (½ cup) whipped heavy cream
- 3½ (½ cup) hazelnuts (roasted)
- 2 oz. (¼ cup) white chocolate (shaved)

How to make them:

1. To begin, add the sugar to the water and bring to a boil.
2. Meanwhile, separate the egg yolks into a bowl and whisk them together then slowly melt the white chocolate in a *double boiler*.
3. When the internal temperature of the boiling sugar and water reaches 230° F. (110° C) when tested with a candy thermometer remove from the heat. Gradually add the sugar and water mixture to the beaten egg yolks, whisking to combine. Add the cooled melted white chocolate and continue to whisk until custard is cool.
4. Whip the heavy cream until *soft peaks* appear and gently fold in the custard and the Irish cream liqueur until fully incorporated.
5. Pour into small moulds or small ramekin dishes and freeze.
6. To make the cookies, place the butter and sugar into a saucepan and slowly melt on medium-high heat. Preheat oven to 320 F.
7. Stir in the golden cane syrup and mix to combine with a wooden spoon.
8. Remove from the heat then add the flour and ginger. Leave mixture to cool.
9. Roll into small ¾" balls and place each one onto a pan lined with non-stick baking paper 4" apart and bake for 10 minutes or until the cookies are a dark golden color.
10. Remove cookies from the oven and leave to cool slightly before removing from pan with a fish slice.
11. To assemble, decorate the plate with a chocolate drizzle then remove the frozen pudding from the mould and gently place a brandy snap cookie on top. Spoon a little freshly whipped cream on top of the cookie and garnish with white chocolate shavings and scatter a few roasted hazelnuts around outside of plate.

Banoffee pie with a southern pecan crust
banana and toffee pie with fresh whipped cream and chocolate shavings

The story:

This scrumptious pie was first invented in an English restaurant in 1972. Its fame spread quickly throughout the British Isles and today it is still incredibly popular throughout Ireland and the UK. Of course, Southerners just *love* pies too, so I have created an Irish-Southern hybrid here by adding a crunchy Southern pecan crust in their honor. The original recipe for the toffee was to boil a tin of sweetened condensed milk for 4 hours in a saucepan of water, checking every 30 minutes to see if the water needs replenishing. Here, though, I have taken a slightly different route, which I think you will prefer and which gives excellent results without all that boiling. Serve this with a nice rich cup of coffee and you'll have a marriage made in heaven!

Banoffee pie ingredients (serves 8–10 people):

(For the pecan crust)
- 8 oz. (2 cups) graham crackers or Irish digestive biscuits (crushed)
- 1 Tbsp. fine granulated sugar
- 2 oz. (½ cup) pecans (finely chopped)
- 4 oz. (½ cup) melted butter

(For the toffee layer)
- 4 oz. (½ cup) butter
- 4 oz. fine granulated sugar
- 24 fl. oz. (2 cups) sweetened condensed milk
- pinch of kosher salt

(For the filling)
- 3 medium bananas
- 4 fl. oz. (½ cup) heavy whipping cream
- 1 tsp. fine granulated sugar
- 1 Tbsp. grated milk chocolate (to garnish)

How to make it:
1. To make the crust, combine all ingredients together in a bowl then press the crumb mixture into the bottom of a large greased 9" pie plate.
2. Bake the crust for 10 minutes at 325° F. Cool and set aside.
3. To make the toffee, combine the butter, sugar, and sweetened condensed milk in a small saucepan. Stir until melted and then bring to a slow boil.
4. Cook toffee for 15 minutes or until the toffee thickens and changes to a rich caramel color. *(Remember to stir all the time, as mixture can easily burn.)* Remove from heat and beat for 2 minutes.
5. Pour toffee over the prepared crust.
6. To prevent bananas from turning brown, pour boiling water over the unpeeled bananas. *(Amazingly, the skins will go black, but this will prevent the fruit inside from browning!)*
7. Whisk fresh cream and sugar in electric mixer until *soft peaks* appear.
8. Peel the bananas and slice. Arrange the sliced bananas over the toffee and finish with a generous dollop of fresh whipped cream.
9. Garnish with chocolate shavings.

Dunluce Castle, County Antrim

Ardboe High Cross, County Tyrone

Antebellum finery, Roswell Georgia

Georgia Dogwoods in bloom

Irish-Southern fusion

Irish–Southern fusion, a blending of the old with the new. A fusing of Southern ingredients and ideas with Irish techniques and traditions. The best of both worlds!

Leganany Dolmen, County Down, Northern Ireland

The Giant's Causeway, County Antrim

Southern Magnolias

Irish-Southern Fusion: Two Worlds Collide

As you have discovered so far in this book, the North of Ireland and the Southern states of America are just brimming over with similarities, most of which are historical and cultural. Created by centuries of Scots-Irish immigration to the South, many overlaps exist in the arts, music, community, ethics, and faith. However, yet another similarity exists, found in the wealth of locally grown produce available in each region—music to the ears of any cook, as you'll discover.

As I've celebrated in earlier chapters, I grew up on a farm in Northern Ireland, surrounded by the deep green fields of rural Ulster that have long been the farmstead of Europe. The roaming, hormone-free livestock eat lush green grass fed by the rain-soaked Irish climate, not the grain feeds of many other places. Patchwork fields are filled with potatoes, carrots, turnips, peas, beans, and many other green goodies, while age-old orchards dot the landscape of County Armagh, where I spent my childhood.

And so it is with Georgia, a state whose climate lends itself to all manner of produce being grown on farms across the land. Peanuts, pecans, pumpkins, apples, sweet onions, and, of course, soft, round peaches are famous for their quality throughout the United States and the world, as are the pork products that inspire many a back-deck barbequing, along with the literally millions of chickens raised in Georgia each and every year. So, as a cook it was a joy to move from one agricultural treasure trove to another. I have always believed that locally grown produce, fresh from the farm and as natural as possible, makes for the tastiest food. To be creative in the kitchen you need only put a little research into what is good where and, most importantly, when. In other words, *cook in season*, and you'll never go wrong.

Granted, it took me years to appreciate the rich rural heritage of Georgia for the wonderful resource that it truly is. When we moved to the South, we moved to the city of Atlanta, where many folks could live out their entire lives and have no exposure to the land or to the origins of their food at all. But after several years of living in the metro area, I had a desire to seek out the beauty of rural Georgia, to discover all that lies beyond the I-285 Atlanta perimeter and what I found truly inspired me as a cook. I became fascinated with what seemed to me to be an unusual manner of farming, with the huge tree farms that grew delicious pecans and peaches, and the sprawling livestock and chicken farms. These seemed so odd to me, being used to the small green patchwork of Irish farms, but I was nonetheless greatly impressed with the dedication of these farms and the produce they created—so much so, that it occurred to me to somehow combine the produce grown in each region into recipes that would fuse the best of each world. We already have fusion and overlaps in music and the arts, so why not in food? To most this may seem a little far-fetched, but it came somewhat natural to me. Why not use Georgia pecans in a traditionally Irish trout dish? Or peaches with an old Ulster favorite such as rhubarb? Or Irish whiskey flavors with Georgia-grown chicken?

There is just something appealing about combining the old traditions with the New World produce grown in the South. After all, I am sure the Scots-Irish immigrants of the eighteenth century did just that. As they moved into Appalachia, the new landscape, climate, and soil conditions would have forced them to improvise with squash and sweet potatoes in place of the old familiar Irish root vegetables they left behind. I'm sure they experimented with the beans or wild fruits cultivated by the Creek Indians, and in may ways I'm just reliving those experiences, only this time in the twenty-first century with all the modern conveniences that our kitchens bring.

So I hope you will have as much fun as I have had discovering just what can be achieved by combining Old World recipes and techniques with New World flavors: Irish-Southern fusion—and the journey has never tasted better!

APPLe & Zucchini Soup
with crispy pancetta, curried pecans, and crème fraiche

The Story:

I created this soup dish for a Regional Chef's Dinner in Perry, Georgia, and it's been one of my favorites ever since. The event was sponsored by the Georgia Apple and Pecan Growers Association, and each chef was challenged to use his creativity by utilizing the quality produce on hand, to make their own signature dish. This recipe was *my* creation at that challenge, and I'm glad to say that it went down very well at the event. I felt the flavors all complemented each other very well. The apple and zucchini (or *courgettes*, as they are known in Ireland) balanced each other very well, giving it a robust flavor with a hint of sweetness, while the curried pecans added that unexpected kick, making this soup a memorable starting dish.

Apple and zucchini soup ingredients (serves 6):

- 2 Tbsp. butter
- 2 small onions (1½ cups) chopped
- 3 large zucchini squash (18 oz.)(peeled and chopped)
- 3 Granny Smith apples (2 cups) (peeled and chopped)
- 1 medium potato (½ cup) (peeled and chopped)
- 1½ pints (3 cups) vegetable stock
- 1 tsp. sea salt
- pinch of white pepper
- 1 tsp. curry powder
- ¼ tsp. cinnamon
- ¼ tsp. nutmeg
- 2 fl. oz. (¼ cup) apple juice
- 2 fl. oz. (¼ cup) heavy whipping cream

Garnish ingredients:

- 1 oz. (¼ cup) curried pecans (see recipe)
- 2 fl. oz. (¼ cup) crème fraiche
- squeeze of lemon juice
- pinch of salt
- 3 slices pancetta (fried crisp and chopped)

How to make it:

1. In a large soup pot, melt the butter and sauté the onions over a medium to low heat, then cover and cook until they are soft but translucent. Takes about 5–7 minutes.
2. Add the zucchini and potato and sauté those with onions for a further 5 minutes until they are tender.
3. Add the stock, curry powder, cinnamon, nutmeg, and salt and simmer for 10 minutes.
4. Add the chopped apples and cook for another 7–10 minutes until *all* the ingredients are tender.
5. Remove the soup from the boil and allow it to cool slightly.
6. Purée the soup in a food processor or handheld blender in batches.
7. Return the soup to the pot and stir in the apple juice. Place over low heat and simmer for a further 5 minutes until heated through.
8. Stir in the cream and continue to simmer for a few minutes, stirring frequently until heated through. Taste and adjust seasoning as necessary.
9. Serve into individual warmed bowls.
10. To prepare the garnish, squeeze a little lemon juice and add a pinch of salt to the crème fraiche in a small bowl.
11. Fry off the pancetta in a skillet until crispy for about 1 minute on each side.
12. Transfer the crème fraiche mixture to a squeeze bottle.
13. Serve into individual warmed bowls and dot small circles on the soup with the crème fraiche, using a toothpick to form a swirl.
14. Chop the pancetta and then sprinkle in the center of the soup, along with 1 tsp. of curried pecans.

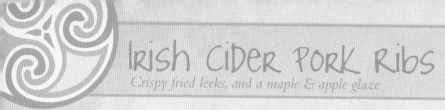

Irish Cider Pork Ribs
Crispy fried leeks, and a maple & apple glaze

The Story:

Our childhoods were spent surrounded by apple orchards, and we were delighted to discover that Georgia has its very own orchard country in Ellijay in the Georgia Mountains. To create a fusion of cultures, I combined the apple with maple for the glaze, which works wonders for the pork.

Cider ribs & crispy leeks ingredients:

- 2½ lbs. pork loin back ribs or pork spare-ribs (cut in pieces)
- ½ tsp. kosher salt
- ¼ tsp. ground black pepper
- 2 Tbsp. vegetable oil
- 6 fl. oz. (¾ cup) Irish or English apple cider
- 4 fl. oz. (½ cup) chicken stock
- 1 small leek (white root and part of the green only)
- 2 Tbsp. cornstarch
- 2 Tbsp. all-purpose flour
- ¼ tsp. sea salt

Maple apple glaze ingredients:

- 2 Tbsp. shallots (chopped)
- 1 Tbsp. butter
- 8 fl. oz. (1 cup) apple cider
- 4 fl. oz. (½ cup) white wine
- 2 Tbsp. apple cider vinegar
- 4 oz. (½ cup) brown sugar
- 2 Tbsp. maple syrup
- 1 cinnamon stick
- ¼ tsp. black pepper

Apple potato mash ingredients:

- 2½ lbs. potatoes (peeled and cut)
- 3 Granny Smith apples (peeled, cored, sliced)
- 6 fl. oz. (¾ cup) water
- 1 tsp. kosher salt
- ¼ tsp. white pepper
- 6 Tbsp. butter
- 2 fl. oz. (¼ cup) heavy whipping cream
- 2 fl. oz. (¼ cup) chicken stock

How to make them:

1. Preheat the oven to 300° F. Score the bone side of the ribs with a sharp knife then season them with salt and pepper.
2. In a large skillet, braise the ribs in oil on a medium-high heat for 4 minutes on each side until they're a golden brown color.
3. Remove ribs from pan and transfer to prepared baking pan.
4. Deglaze the pan with apple cider and chicken stock. Cover tightly with foil, piercing a few holes for evaporation, and bake for 2½ hours.
5. While ribs are in the oven, prepare maple apple glaze by placing butter in a small saucepan and sautéing shallots for 1 minute to soften. Add remaining ingredients and simmer for about 30 minutes or until liquid has been reduced by two thirds. Strain into small bowl.
6. Remove ribs from cooking liquid and cool. Cut each rib with sharp knife and transfer to a baking tray.
7. Wash leeks and then cut in half lengthwise. Cut in thin 2" strips. Toss in cornstarch, flour, and salt. Heat oil in deep fat fryer or in skillet with 2" of vegetable oil and fry until crispy but still retaining green color.
8. Before serving, transfer the ribs to a baking dish and bake at 325° F. Brush warmed maple apple glaze over the ribs.
9. Allow 4 ribs per person and garnish with a small handful of crispy fried leeks.

Golden Fried Goat's Cheese Salad
with Georgia peaches, pecans, and an Earl Grey dressing

The story:

The smoky, orange bergamot overtones of Earl Grey tea infused into the dressing of this dish bring together the superb Southern flavors of peaches, pecans, and fried goat's cheese in almost perfect harmony. Delicious and elegant as a starter or as a light lunch option on a warm, sunny day, this dish pairs well with chilled oaky chardonnays and good conversations!

Goat's cheese salad ingredients:

- 2 oz. (½ cup) pecan halves
- 1 Tbsp. butter
- 1 tsp. sugar
- pinch of kosher salt
- 1 (6 oz.) log of goat's cheese (cut into 8 medallions)
- salt and pepper (to season)
- 2 Tbsp. flour
- 1 egg (beaten with 1 Tbsp. milk)
- 3½ oz. (½ cup) breadcrumbs
- vegetable oil (to fry)
- 2 peaches
- 2 oz. (1 cup) organic micro greens (pea sprouts)

Earl Grey tea vinaigrette ingredients:

- 4 fl. oz (½ cup) sherry vinegar
- 3 Punjana Earl Grey teabags
- 2 small shallots (finely minced)
- zest and juice of one small orange
- 1 tsp. Dijon mustard
- 1 tsp. sugar
- 1 Tbsp. honey
- 8 fl. oz. (1 cup) oil (½ canola and ½ olive oil)
- kosher salt and freshly ground black pepper to taste

How to make it:

1. Begin by toasting the pecans in a skillet with butter and salt, stirring all the time until lightly toasted. Be careful not to burn! Set aside to cool on a piece of greaseproof paper.
2. Prepare the vinaigrette by bringing the sherry vinegar to boiling point and pour over the Earl Grey teabags to steep for 3–5 minutes in a suitable container.
3. Remove teabags and discard and allow the infused vinegar to cool.
4. Combine the vinegar with the orange juice and zest, shallots, honey, sugar, mustard, salt, and pepper. Slowly whisk in the oils until incorporated. Taste to adjust seasoning. Refrigerate.
5. In three separate bowls prepare the dipping ingredients: first the beaten egg and milk, second the breadcrumbs, and last the flour.
6. Season the goat's cheese medallions with a little salt and pepper.
7. Dip the goat's cheese into the flour first to prevent sticking. Then follow by dipping the cheese into the egg wash and finally into the prepared breadcrumbs. When done, chill in the refrigerator for 30 minutes.
8. Peel the peaches and cut in half to remove the stone. Using a paring knife, follow the natural curvature of the fruit to cut slices. Set aside.
9. Heat at least ½" of vegetable oil in skillet and bring to medium hot. Fry the goat's cheese for 1–2 minutes on each side, carefully turning for evenness.
10. Combine the micro greens and toss them in a little vinaigrette.
11. To serve, place 2 goats' cheese fritters in the center of each plate and top with slices of fresh peaches and organic micro greens. Top with toasted pecans and drizzle over a little of the Earl Grey tea vinaigrette.

Sweet Georgia Pulled Pork & Red Cabbage
with a sweet barbeque sauce on warm Irish-style potato-apple farls

The Story:

Most people just don't have access to a large-scale smoker, so here I have improvised instructions on how to make this dish at home without compromising *too much* on flavor. For an Irish-Southern fusion I have paired the pulled pork with some tangy red cabbage, my own Georgia-style sweet barbeque sauce and present it on Irish potato-apple bread farls.

Southern pulled pork ingredients:

- 2½ lbs. boneless pork shoulder (tie with string)
- salt brine (overnight soak) *(see recipe in The Coming to America chapter for fried chicken)*
- 8 oz. (1 cup) apple juice
- 3 oz. water
- soaked or damp hickory wood chips
- 4 Tbsp. sweet pork dry rub (plus 1 tsp)*(see recipe in the Southern grill chapter for pork chops)*
- Irish whiskey barbeque sauce *(see recipe in Southern Grill chapter for pork chops)*
- Potato apple bread *(see recipe in Irish bakery chapter for potato bread)*

Braised red cabbage ingredients:

- ½ small red cabbage (4 cups) cored and finely shredded
- 12 oz. (1½ cups) water (to blanch)
- 4 oz. (½ cup) red wine vinegar (to blanch)
- 2 Tbsp. olive oil
- 1 small onion (¾ cup)
- 2 cloves garlic (crushed)
- 6 oz. (¾ cups) chicken stock
- 3 Tbsp. apple cider vinegar
- ¼ tsp. coarse salt
- 1 tsp. thyme (chopped)
- ¼ tsp. freshly ground black pepper
- 2½ Tbsp. sugar

How to make it:

1. To prepare the pork, first soak it overnight in salt brine.
2. Preheat your oven to 475° F.
3. Score the fatty side of the pork with a knife and massage 4 Tbsp. of pork rub all over the meat.
4. Place the pork on a roasting rack fat side up and bake for 30 minutes on high.
5. After 30 minutes, add the apple juice and water and cover the pork with foil. Switch the heat down to 250° F and bake for a further 5–7 hours until the meat is falling apart. Reserve the cooking liquid.
6. To try and replicate the delicious smoky flavor of the meat, place some slightly damp hickory oak wood chips in punctured foil packets in a gas barbeque and grill the meat for about 5 minutes on each side when the wood begins to smoke slightly. Or, scatter damp hickory chips into an already hot charcoal barbeque to create the smoke, before grilling.
7. While meat is cooking, prepare the potato apple bread *(see the "Irish Bakery" chapter for recipe)* and the braised red cabbage.
8. To prepare the braised red cabbage, bring some cold water and red wine vinegar to a boil in a medium-sized saucepan and blanch the cabbage for about 10 seconds. Then drain the cabbage off.
9. In another large pan heat the olive oil and sauté the onion until tender. Add garlic and sauté for another minute.
10. Add the cabbage and chicken stock and cook for a further 5 minutes.
11. Add the apple cider vinegar, sugar, salt, pepper, and thyme and cook for 5 more minutes, stirring constantly. Set aside.
12. Finely chop the pork or pull apart with fingers. Stir in 3–4 fluid oz of reserved cooking liquid and 1 tsp. of the dry pork rub mixture.
13. To assemble dish, arrange a triangle of potato-apple bread on the plate, top it with the pulled pork and a drizzle of barbeque sauce, and finish with the braised red cabbage on top.
14. Garnish with a sprig of thyme.

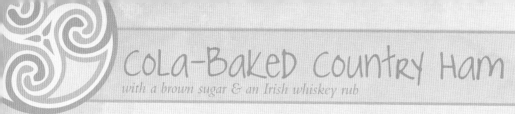

Cola-Baked Country Ham
with a brown sugar & an Irish whiskey rub

The Story:

Atlanta's favorite drink combined with some brown sugar and Irish whiskey produces the tastiest results you could imagine and may be the best baked ham I have ever eaten. I know you will find this hard to believe, but the flavors are a favorable marriage, making a Southern style country baked ham with an Irish twist that will keep your guests coming back for more. The story alone is good entertainment for your guests!

A friend of mine gave me the tip about using cola as a means of basting the ham to bring out the flavor, and despite some misgivings I originally had, it works! The brown sugar and Irish whiskey rub came a bit more naturally to me, but again, it's the marriage of the two methods that works wonders here, so give it a try!

Cola-baked country ham ingredients:

- 10–12 lb. ham (bone-in)
- 2 (12 fl. oz.) cans of cola

Brown sugar whiskey rub ingredients:

- 1 tsp. coarse sea salt
- 1 tsp. ground cloves
- 8 oz. (1 cup) dark brown sugar
- 2 Tbsp. prepared spicy wholegrain mustard
- 2 fl. oz. (¼ cup). Irish whiskey

How to make it:

1. Preheat oven to 350° F.
2. Use a sharp knife to score surface of the skin of the ham in a crisscross pattern about 1" apart and around ½" deep.
3. Place the ham, fat side up, in a large roasting pan.
4. Combine the brown sugar-whiskey rub ingredients together in a bowl and rub liberally over the surface of the ham.
5. Place the ham in the oven and bake for 30 minutes until the brown sugar melts.
6. Remove the ham from oven and reduce the oven temperature to 325° F.
7. Pour the cola over the ham and then return the ham to the oven, baking for about 20–25 minutes per pound.
8. Continue to baste the ham with the cola and whiskey rub pan juices every 20 minutes or so to give it a nice brown glaze and crispy skin.
9. When done, remove the ham from oven and allow it to rest for at least 10 minutes before transferring to a platter to carve and serve.

Scarlett O'Hara's Shrimp and Grits

The Story:

Chef Samantha Enzemen, owner of the Mercantile Restaurant in Atlanta, is famous for her *Shrimp and Grits* and the stories she tells in the kitchen. Samantha herself says: "The South was founded on the sweat, love, and toil of hardworking immigrants. For most of Georgia, our people came from Ireland, Scotland, and England. As a Southern girl I can't think of a more fitting tribute to Katie Scarlett O'Hara than to incorporate Irish butter and cheese into The Mercantile's Shrimp and Grits. *Erin Go Bragh!*"

Chef Samantha Enzemen

Ingredients: (recipe to serve 4 people)

- 2½ fl. oz. (1/3 cups) cooked grits (per serving)
- 2 oz. (¼ cup) unsalted butter (plus 3 Tbsp. to finish)
- 2 Tbsp. vegetable oil
- 28 Georgia White Shrimp (21–24 count peeled and de-veined)
- 1 Tbsp. Creole seasoning
- 4 fl. oz. (½ cup) Sauce Creole (see below)
- 6 fl. oz. (¾ cup) heavy cream

(For the garnish)

- crispy bacon crumbles
- scallions (bias cut)
- parsley (rough chop)

(For the cheese grits)

- 12 fl. oz. (1½ cups) water
- 12 fl. oz. (1½ cups) milk
- 8 fl. oz. (1 cup) of Plantation white speckled grits
- 8 fl. oz. (1 cup) heavy cream
- 2 oz. (¼ cup) unsalted butter
- 6 oz. (1½ cups) aged Irish cheddar cheese
- 3 green onions (4 Tbsp. bias cut)

(For the Sauce Creole)

- 2 oz. unsalted butter
- ¼ lb. bacon (cut into 1" pieces)
- 1 large onion (chopped)
- 1 green bell pepper (cored, seeded, and chopped)
- 3 stalks of celery (chopped fine)
- 1 Tbsp. Creole seasoning
- 4 cloves of garlic (minced)
- 6 fl. oz. (¾ cups) white wine
- 5 oz. canned tomatoes
- 2 bay leaves

How to make the sauce:

1. In a rondeau over a medium heat melt the butter and then add the bacon and cook until slightly crisp, about 10 minutes.
2. In the food processor, process the tomatoes to take them from whole to crushed.
3. Add the onions, green peppers, and celery and cook until onions are translucent.
4. Add the garlic and stir for 30 seconds, then add the Creole seasoning and increase the heat to high and cook for 1 minute longer.
5. Add the white wine and deglaze the pan, scraping up any remnants from bacon or onions on the bottom of the pan.
6. Reduce the wine by ½ then add the tomatoes. Stir to incorporate. Add the bay leaves and simmer for 20–30 minutes. Taste and adjust seasonings as necessary.

How to make the shrimp and grits:

1. Add a serving of cooked grits per bowl.
2. In a large skillet, add the butter and the oil and melt over high heat.
3. In a medium bowl sprinkle the shrimp with the Creole seasoning, tossing the shrimp to coat and season thoroughly.
4. Add the shrimp to the skillet and cook, shaking the pan to prevent shrimp from sticking, then ladle the Creole sauce into the pan once the shrimp are pink on both sides but not finished cooking.
5. Add the heavy cream to the sauce and shrimp and swirl the pan to incorporate the remaining 3 Tbsp. of butter and swirl until melted.
6. Ladle the sauce over the shrimp and check the shrimp to ensure they are cooked through.
7. Plate 7 shrimp each atop the portioned grits and nappé the sauce over the grits and shrimp.
8. Garnish with bacon crumbles, scallions, and parsley.

Irish Stout-Braised Short Ribs
served with Georgia peanuts, shallots, and garden herbs on a bed of Irish "Champ" potatoes

The Story:

Being an Irish cook, my busiest time of year is naturally middle March when we celebrate dear ol' St. Patrick. People across this great land just *love* to celebrate all things Irish on Saint Patrick's Day, and the Irish pubs and restaurants are filled to overflowing with patrons seeking *something* with an Irish theme to go with their stout or green beer.

This recipe comes from a signature dish I was asked to create for Murphy's Restaurant in Atlanta, to place on their menu *just* for St. Patrick's night. The dish was a huge success, and the braised beef, falling off the bone with overtones of rich Irish stout, is bound to please anyone. Georgia peanuts and local Southern greens were added for a "fusion" flavor.

Irish stout-braised ribs ingredients (serves 4):

- 4½ lbs. beef short ribs (bone-in)
- 1 tsp. kosher salt
- ½ tsp. black pepper
- 2 Tbsp. vegetable oil
- 1 oz. (¼ cup) all-purpose flour
- 2 Tbsp. unsalted butter
- 1 large onion (chopped)
- 2 medium carrots (chopped)
- 2 stalk celery (chopped)
- 2 Granny Smith apples (chopped)
- bouquet garni (bunch of thyme & bay leaf tied together)
- 1½ pints (3 cups) veal stock
- 1½ pints (3 cups) chicken stock
- one 12 oz. bottle of Irish stout
- 2 fl. oz. (¼ cup) molasses

Garnish ingredients:

- garden herbs (chervil, chives, parsley)
- 1½ oz (¼ cup) Georgia peanuts (roasted and chopped)
- 1 oz. (¼ cup) pickled shallots (chopped)

How to make it:

1. Season the ribs with salt and pepper and toss them in flour.
2. Heat some oil in a large skillet and braise the ribs over a medium-high heat for 4 minutes on each side to *seal*, then transfer to a large baking pan.
3. Sauté the onions, carrots, celery, and apple in a skillet until softened then transfer to the same large baking pan with the ribs.
4. Pour over the Irish stout, stocks, and molasses. Stir and add the bouquet garni.
5. Place the baking pan in the lower third of the oven at 250° for 4–5 hours until the beef is tender and falling off the bone.
6. Strain the cooking liquid and set aside and discard the vegetables and bouquet garni.
7. Transfer the cooked ribs to a cooling rack and remove the meat from the bones.
8. In a skillet pan, reduce the braising liquid to half by slowly simmering.
9. Combine rib meat with the sauce to finish.
10. Serve the braised short ribs on a bed of green "Champ" potatoes (see the "Heritage" chapter) garnished with local herbs, roasted Georgia peanuts, and some pickled shallots.
11. Enjoy with your favorite Irish brew, and toast ol' St. Patrick!

The Irish Plough Boy in a Jar

*with an apple and celery salad infused with walnut vinaigrette, apple chutney, aged Irish cheddar cheese,
and toasted wheaten bread crumble*

The Story:

This most interesting of fusion delights comes from two traditions. The "jar" is of course a Southern tradition that goes back generations where everything was "put in a jar." The tradition even extends to the modern era with Southern sweet tea; ask for sweet tea in a traditional Southern restaurant and the beverage *may* arrive in a pickle jar, *not* in a conventional glass!

As for the salad itself, this is a traditional Irish dish—The Ploughman's Lunch—which derives its name from the "brown bag lunch" created for farm hands working in the soft Irish fields. So, I have taken the two and fused them together for a practical and interesting lunch idea!

Irish Plough Boy ingredients (serves 4):

- 4 fl. oz. (½ cup) apple chutney (see below)
- 1 Granny Smith apple (cored & diced with skins on)
- 1 Red Delicious apple (cored & diced with skins on)
- 2 stalks of celery (scraped and diced)
- 4 Tbsp. (¼ cup) walnut vinaigrette (see below)
- 6 oz. (1½ cups) aged Irish cheddar cheese (grated)
- 4 slices of Irish wheaten bread (crumbled and toasted)
- 2 Tbsp. butter
- 2 tsp. thyme, sage, parsley (chopped)

Walnut vinaigrette ingredients:

- 5 Tbsp. white wine vinegar
- 3 Tbsp. lemon juice
- ½ tsp. kosher salt
- ½ tsp. white pepper
- 4 fl. oz. (½ cup) walnut oil
- 4 fl. oz. (½ cup) vegetable oil
- 2 Tbsp. sugar

Apple Chutney ingredients:

- 4 lbs. Granny Smith apples (peeled, cored, chopped)
- 3 oz. (½ cup) golden raisins
- 1 lb. Vidalia onions (peeled and chopped)
- 1 lb. soft brown sugar
- 14 fl. oz. (1 ¾ cups) cider vinegar
- 2 fl. oz. (¼ cup) lemon juice
- ½ tsp. salt
- ¼ tsp. white pepper
- 1 tsp. ginger (minced)
- 1 tsp. ground cinnamon
- ¼ tsp. ground cloves
- ¼ tsp. ground nutmeg

How to make it:

1. Make the apple chutney by combining all the ingredients in a large saucepan and cook on medium high.

2. When the chutney is boiling, turn the heat down to medium low and simmer for 1½ hours, stirring occasionally with a wooden spoon.

3. Allow the chutney to cool completely. (If making in advance, follow canning guidelines and place in sealed jars).

4. Next, prepare the vinaigrette by mixing the apple cider vinegar, lemon juice, sugar, celery seed salt, white pepper, walnut oil, and vegetable oil together in a large glass jar. Then seal the jar and *shake well* to combine.

5. For the jar contents, crumble the bread and toss it in melted butter and herbs.

6. Place the crumbs on a large baking tray and toast in the oven at 350° for 5–6 minutes until brown and crunchy. Remove from the oven and cool.

7. Chop the apples and celery and combine in large bowl.

8. Toss the salad in the walnut vinaigrette.

9. To layer the salad in the jar, begin with apple and celery salad, placing those at the bottom, then layer in the apple chutney, followed by more apple and celery salad, then vintage cheddar, and end with toasted wheaten bread crumbles on top.

10. Serve or refrigerate for a great and mobile lunch option at any time!

Spiced Meringue with Brown Bread Pecan Ice Cream
with sharp apple crisps

The Story:

Each October many Southerners make their way to the highlands of Appalachia to indulge in the seasonal love affair with the apples that ripen in autumn. This wonderful dessert brings several mouthwatering textures together with light marshmallow meringue, sweet cake crumb, spiced apples, and creamy brown bread and pecan ice cream served with crunchy apple crisps for your fall enjoyment.

Spiced apple meringue ingredients:

(For the base)
- 7 oz. (2 cups) cake crumbs
- 2 oz. (¼ cup) butter

(For the apple filling)
- 3 large cooking apples (peeled, cored, and sliced)
- 3 Tbsp. orange juice
- 1½ oz. (¼ cup) brown sugar
- pinch of ground cloves
- pinch of nutmeg
- ½ tsp. cinnamon

(For the meringue)
- 3 egg whites
- ½ tsp. vanilla extract
- ¼ tsp. cream of tartar
- 2½ oz. (1/3 cup) sugar

(For the apple crisps)
- 1 Granny Smith apple
- pinch of cinnamon (for dusting)

Easy brown bread and pecan ice cream ingredients:
- 22 fluid oz. (2¾ cups) sweetened condensed milk
- 2 pints (4 cups) heavy whipping cream
- 1 tsp. vanilla
- 5 oz. (1½ cups) brown soda breadcrumbs
- 3 Tbsp. brown sugar
- 2½ oz. (½ cup) toasted pecans

How to make it:

1. Make the apple crisps ahead of time by peeling and slicing a whole apple thinly, showing the central star shape in the core of the apple. Then place on a cookie sheet and bake in a very low oven of 140° for 2 hours until dry and crisp.
2. Melt the butter in a large pan, place the cake crumbs in the pan, and gently allow the cake crumbs to brown lightly.
3. Spoon the resulting crumb mixture into 6 buttered ramekin dishes and set aside.
4. Next, slice the apples and place them in a medium heavy-based saucepan with the orange juice, sugar, cloves, and cinnamon.
5. Cover and simmer gently for 10 minutes until the apples are soft, then remove from the heat and spoon the apples on top of the cake crumb mixture.
6. Beat the egg whites, vanilla, and cream of tartar at high speed with an electric mixer for about 1 minute. Gradually add the sugar 1 Tbsp. at a time and continue beating or until *soft peaks* appear and the sugar dissolves (2–4 minutes).
7. Spoon on top of the apples and bake at 325° for 25–28 minutes.
8. To assemble, place the spiced apple meringue dish on one side of a large dessert plate with brown bread and pecan ice cream and apple crisp on the other end. Dust with a little cinnamon.

How to make easy brown bread and pecan ice cream:

1. Preheat the oven to 350° F. Combine the brown sugar and breadcrumbs on an aluminum foil-lined baking sheet. Bake for 4–5 minutes, stirring occasionally until crumbs are crunchy and caramelized.
2. Beat the cream until it is thick enough to leave a trail behind. Fold in the condensed milk, vanilla, bread crumbs and toasted pecans.
3. Finally, transfer to a container and freeze for 12–24 hours.

For more information about
Judith McLoughlin
&
The Shamrock and Peach
please visit:

www.shamrockandpeach.com
www.shamrockandpeachphoto.com
Facebook: @shamrockandpeach
Twitter: @shamrock_peach
Twitter: @shampeachphoto
Judith@shamrockandpeach.com
gary@shamrockandpeach.com

For more photography by
Gary McLoughlin
please visit:
www.shamrockandpeachphoto.com

....

For more information about
AMBASSADOR INTERNATIONAL
please visit:

www.ambassador-international.com
@AmbassadorIntl
www.facebook.com/AmbassadorIntl